Intermediate Guide to Celtic Patterns

Table of Contents

Introduction

This book—Intermediate Guide to Celtic Patterns—will sharpen your skills, teach you how to use the basic knowledge you already acquired, push you further along the journey, and turn you into a pro in no time. Prepare your mind for several Celtic projects you never knew existed. Since these projects come with easy step-by-step analysis, you can also create your own designs and "up your skills" a bit.

Are you ready? In this book, you will learn how to incorporate your Celtic patterns into calligraphy, how to integrate these patterns to clothing, how to master your Celtic knots, secret grid techniques you can use to sketch your Celtic patterns, how you can design your own Celtic patterns, and how to sketch Celtic maze patterns. Also, by the time you finish this book, you will understand the fundamentals of illuminated manuscripts, and how to create one, as well as how to integrate zoomorphic knotwork animals into your Celtic artwork, how to create a double Celtic knot paracord, a Celtic monkey fist, and a Celtic knot keychain. Other things you'll learn include how to create colorful mandala projects, and how to use pencil colors to draw khala patterns.

Intermediate Guide to Celtic Patterns, like a traveler's compass, offers clear direction on how you can become a pro in Celtic designs in a short time. Your journey to stardom starts here.

Chapter One:
Celtic Calligraphy

Call it "Celtic Calligraphy" or "Celtic Knots" and you are on point. These knots are actually embellishments often used to create unique designs on clothes and other home decorations. Remnants of these knots are everywhere many years after Celtic civilization hit a standstill. Still, more societies are embracing the Celtic culture, and its influence on the modern world is growing out of control. Celtic knots mean many things to many people but this depends on the overriding culture of the place where the knots are used. Some of these knots symbolize loyalty, love, friendship, and faith. With just a thread, people have used Celtic knots to symbolize how life and eternity are intertwined. Celtic knots, being complex decorative designs, have been extensively used to beautify items such as cutlery, clothing, mugs, plates, and jewelry sets.

A look back at ancient history will help us understand what Celtic knots really stand for. Back around 450 A.D., Christians began to influence Celtic civilization by creating Christian manuscripts and artwork that incorporated plants, animals, and humans. Knot patterns were being used to decorate artefacts, illuminated pages, clothes, and other finished items, not just during the mediaeval times for the Gaelic Celts. Often, these patterns went with beautiful and amazing calligraphy. Still, religious people, apart from Christian and Muslim faithfuls, also had Celtic designs that met their needs.

Celtic knot designs can enhance seamless and elaborate fabrics and other finished items. Their well laid out grids, lines, symmetrical patterns, and flowing letterforms could be all you need to make your finished items spectacular. Are you wondering about how to create knot designs as infill for decorative initials? No worries. Celtic knot designs, like other artworks, are shaped by your innate ability and talent, not just basic or historical principles or skills. Fine, you could learn the principles or practice the original skills, but your creative ingenuity determines how far you will go. Power the principles with personal creativity and you will create great knot designs.

Think about the complexity of the Celtic knots you want to create. See what you need to put in place to achieve it. Sure, it is not something you can achieve in a hurry. You need to exercise some patience as you try to work things out. Some knots, if not all, require certain mathematical structures and principles. So, you need to understand how these structures work before you can create an amazing Celtic knot. Take your time to create elaborate and complex knot patterns you want. Are you wondering about the number of hours it would take you to create a Celtic knot? Designing a Celtic knot could take you 30 minutes, one hour, one day, or many weeks, depending on the size of the design, the number of tiny lines you draw per minute, and how long it takes you to color the tiny boxes you have created.

Gradually, as you draw your Celtic designs, you will really enjoy the process because it is a relaxing and meditative activity. Your level of alertness and creativity will determine how well you handle and enjoy the repetitive movements of creating your favorite knots. Scanners and image software can be used to manipulate and reproduce several sections of Celtic knots rapidly, especially when you are in a hurry to create choice Celtic designs. Some people enjoy the action of drawing by hand, while others love to have the help technology can offer. However, if you really want to master Celtic knots, you need to practice drawing them and really understanding how they are composed structurally.

Popular Celtic Knots and What They Stand For

Celtic knots look good. There is no doubt about that. People have been enjoying these knots as early as the 3rd century. Each knot has its peculiar significance and trying to understand or interpret these knots, without adequate records about their unique symbols, could pose a huge challenge. Today, what we know about Celtic knots is determined by how much access to facts we have had. For example, you might have seen a Celtic Knot on stones in burial sites, and conclude that such knots represent faith or unity among certain people. Also, you might have heard people say that some knots could ward off evil spirits. Yes, they could be right because Celtic patterns in tombs usually reference eternal life or eternity. A Celtic knot has a line that runs continuously without an end. Here, I will show you a few well known Celtic Knots and what they symbolize.

1. Celtic Cross: Being a spiritual symbol, the Celtic cross was used in ancient times to reference the Sun God. Soon, Christians began to see the circle around the cross as God's eternal love for men. Several Celtic crosses of the 3rd and 4th centuries still exist in our modern-day world, and these unique crosses now cut across cultures and religions.

2. Trinity Knot: Triquetra, also known as the trinity knot, was used to honor the neo-pagan triple goddess. But lately, Christians have used it for their 'The Father, The Son, and The Holy Spirit' doctrine. Again, Irish jewelry designers and silversmiths have embellished their products with the trinity knot to showcase the everlasting love of the Irish people.

3. Tree of Life: Already the Irish symbol of nature, the tree of life is one of the most popular Celtic knots around the world. Its flowing form represents the balanced and harmonious natural world.

4. Celtic Love Knot: Feel free to call it the Anam Cara knot or the Celtic love knot. Its two intertwined hearts symbolize friendship and

wisdom. It is an infinite pattern and it represents everlasting love.

5. Sailor's Knot: This knot comes with endless loops made up of two woven ropes. Sailors would weave ropes to remember their loved ones just before they started their journey on the open seas. Again, these knots signified a love that would never break.

6. Shield Knot: Celts believed that shield knots could protect them from evil spirits, both at home and on the battlefield. Shield knots could come in circular or square shapes and they have two spiral knots, apart from the spiral and triple spiral knots.

7. Spiral Knot: Spiral knots have varied meanings depending on where you find their engravings, and they could symbolize a journey from the physical world to the after-life, also known as the spiritual life. For example, spiral knots found at grave sites or passage tombs would represent a spiritual passage to the world beyond.

8. Triple Spiral: Triple spiral knots are trinity designs and they usually represent land, sea, and sky, our natural world.

How to Incorporate Celtic Pattern into Calligraphy

There are a few ways to create Celtic patterns, but all the methods are subject to grid layouts and diagonal line placement. So, how do you incorporate your Celtic pattern knowledge into calligraphy? It's easy. Here's how to do it.

Required Materials

- Paper

- 2.5 mm wide fountain pen

- Steady hands

Instructions

Follow these simple steps to incorporate your celtic pattern into calligraphy.

1. Consider the alphabets and try to memorize what they look like. The alphabets share a few features such as a line in the middle and 2 commas on either side, different sides, or on the alphabets. So, before you do anything, take your time to study the alphabet because it can aid the process.

2. Set a nib angle of your pen while you run the calligraphy.

3. Station the angle of your pen while running the calligraphy.

4. Move your pen all at once. Don't lean on it.

Just follow these instructions to do effortless Celtic calligraphy. Be creative. The level of your creativity will determine the beauty of your Celtic patterns. Again, you need to exercise a great deal of patience. It is hard to be creative without patience. So, develop great Celtic knot ideas, and dedicate your time to actualizing your beautiful ideas.

Chapter Summary

- Celtic knots are embellishments used in creating unique designs and clothes.

- Creativity is the sole determinant of how beautiful a Celtic design can be.

- All Celtic knots have natural and spiritual meanings. For example, the trinity knot was a neo-pagan triple goddess but was later used by Christians to represent 'The Father, The Son, and The Holy Spirit.'

In the next chapter you will learn how to use Celtic patterns to embellish your quilts and clothes.↓

Chapter Two:
Celtic Patterns for Needlework Embellishment, Clothing and Quilts

Celtic patterns are very attractive on every fabric. No wonder people around the world continue to use these patterns to decorate and embellish their trousers, skirts, tops, and jewelry. Use these patterns to embellish your fabrics, and feel free to paint, draw, or even sew them onto your fabrics, and you'll surely love the outcome. In this chapter, you'll learn how to incorporate Celtic patterns on your clothing. Always try to learn the basics of anything you want to do— be it needle felting, serging, or needlework embellishments. Draw on your experience with other crafts to bring your skills to the table. You might want to explore free-motion quilting because it is one of the easiest ways to get started.

How to Draw a Celtic Knot Pattern

Celtic knots are beautiful ornate decorative knots. These super attractive knots are without beginning or end but often take elaborate twists and turns, making some people assume that it is difficult to create. I will show you how to draw these knots for your needlework embellishment, clothing, quilts, and other projects. So, ready a pencil, graph paper, a ruler, and a colored pencil as we get into drawing a few Celtic patterns. Ready your mind and focus on the steps I will be sharing with you shortly because Celtic patterns are complicated. You need 100% concentration and consistent practice to be an expert designer of Celtic knots. With the step-by-step analysis provided here and a few screenshots added, you won't have issues perfecting your Celtic patterns.

1. Draw a rectangle of dots at the corners of your graph paper, as shown below. Here, I created 9 by 7 rectangular dots.

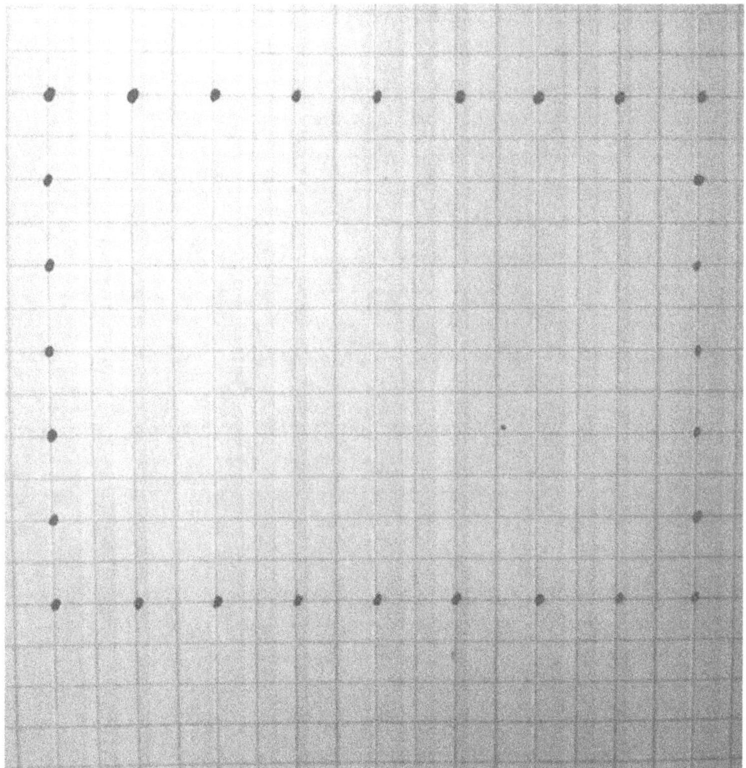

2. Create another set of dots directly under the
   first dots with your colored pencil.

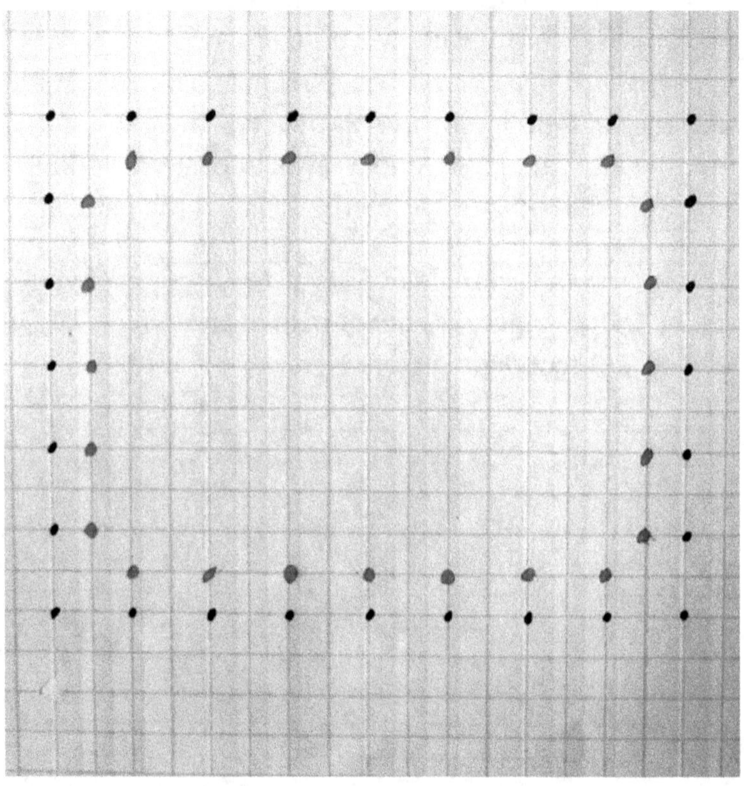

3. Connect the colored dots with your ruler to
   create diagonal lines.

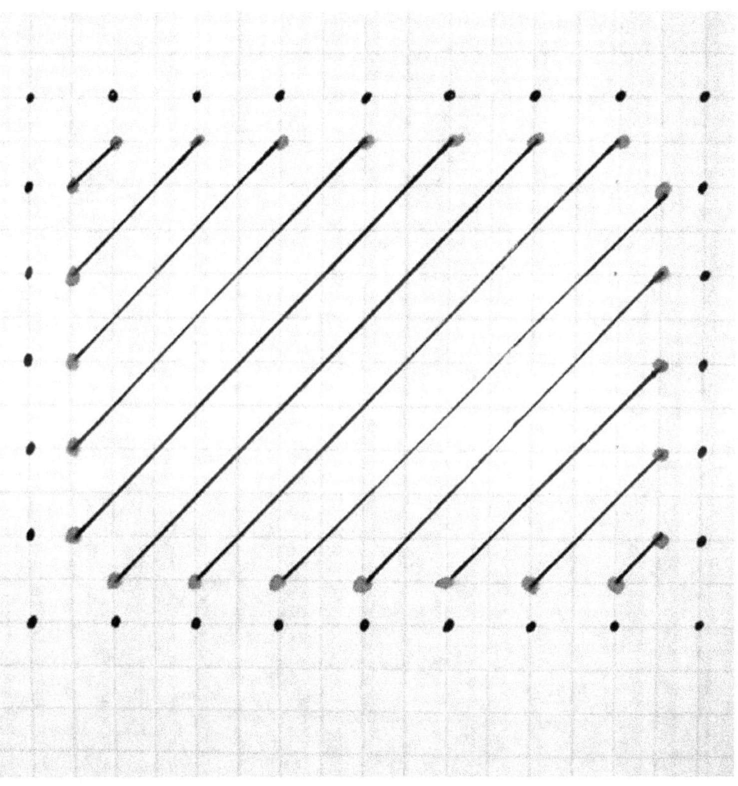

4. Connect the colored dots on the opposite side
   to create a grid filling

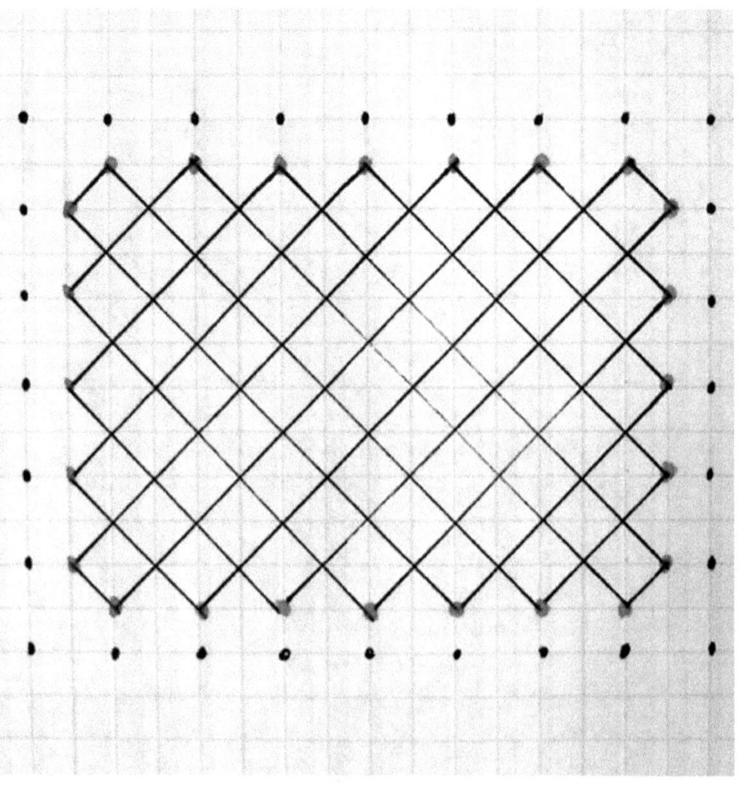

5. Draw the outer edge.

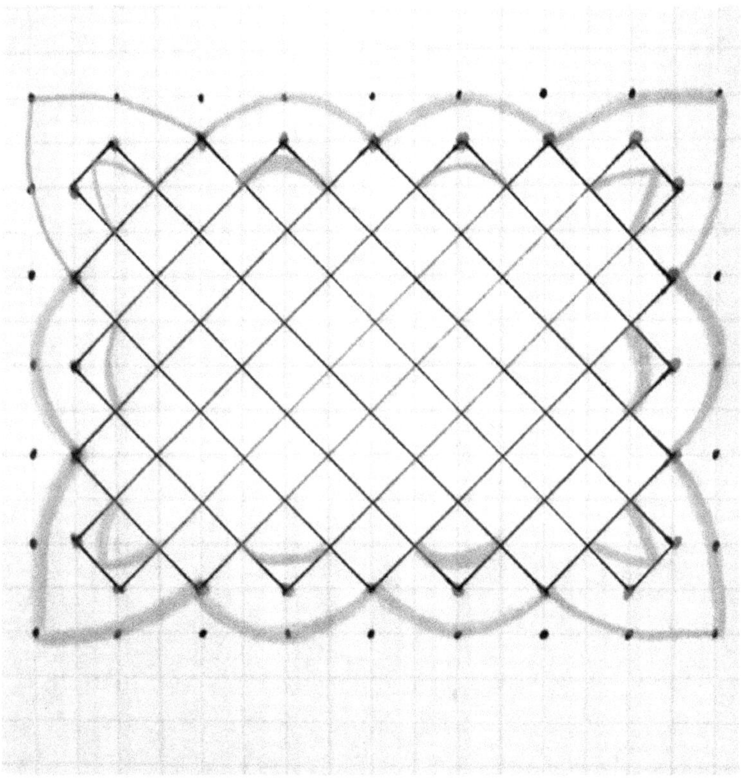

I used a different colored pencil to draw these
new lines so that you could see them clearly. So, try to
draw the lines with your own pencil. Start from the 4
corners and link the line from your second colored dot
to the second pencil dot and the outside corner dot.
Allow this line to connect the second pencil dot and
the second colored dot. Next, draw inner curves or
corners under all the newly created lines. Confused?
It's hard to explain this step with words but no
worries. Just pay keen attention to the image.

6. Clean up the unused hard corners or curves.

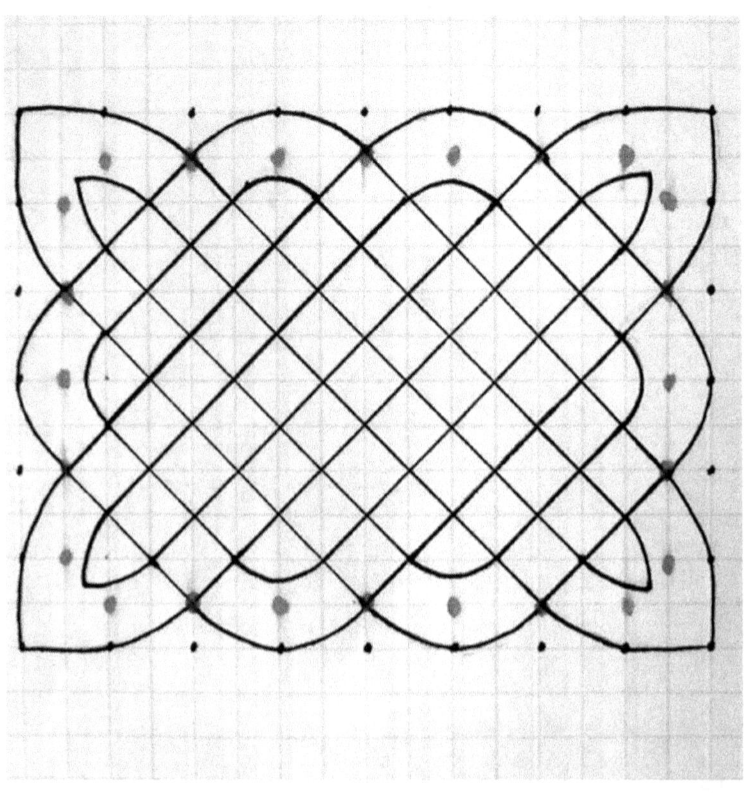

7. Begin to weave the lines.

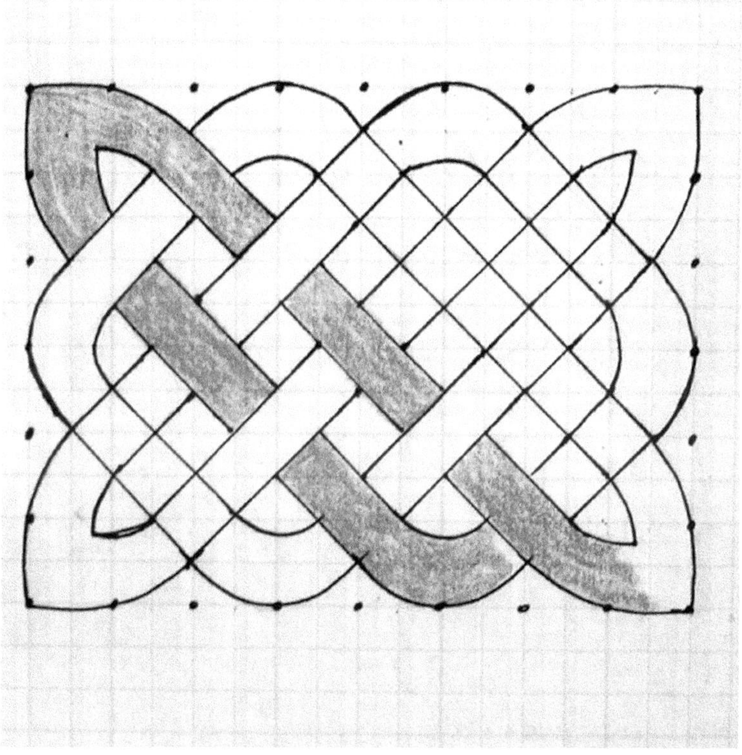

Here, I decided to add color so that you could easily see exactly what I was doing. You only need to erase some lines. Pay attention to how I erased a few lines to create some enticing weaving effects. Continue weaving until you clean up all the lines and get back to where you actually started from.

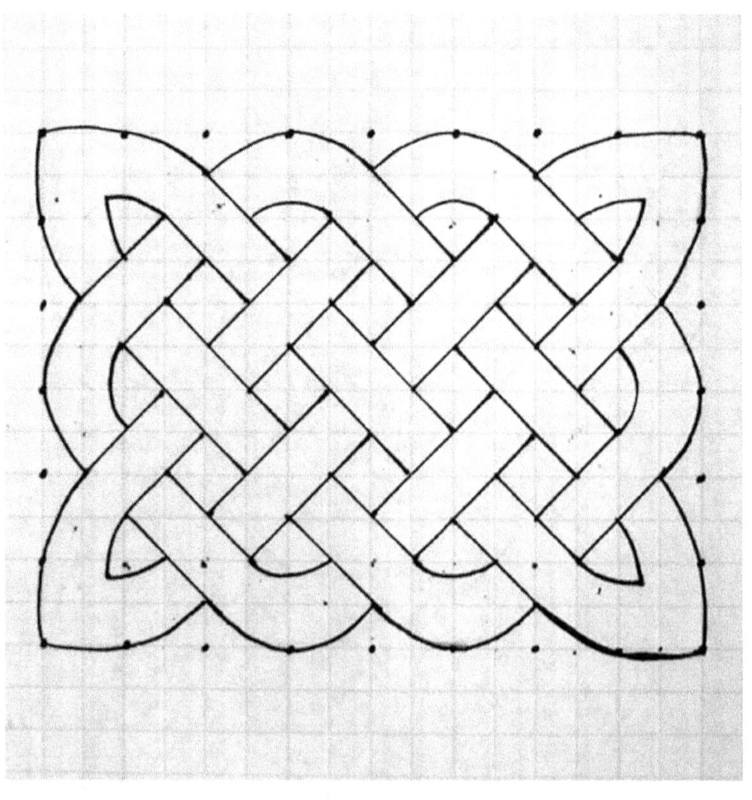

How to Dress Celtic

Celtic knot patterns are so unique and beautiful that most people go for clothes and jewelry adorned with these lovely knots. No wonder the number of people asking for Celtic designs around the world is always on the increase. Some people adopt Celtic attire because of their love for unique and beautiful clothes or just to connect with their ancestors. One thing you just can't ignore about the Celtic lifestyle is the beauty of their knot patterns. Here are a few things to note before you can adopt the perfect Celtic dressing lifestyle.

1. Research clothing styles: Take your time to see a few images of Celtic artistic depictions to know the ones that work for you. It is not just seeing the images. You need to study them and opt for the styles that suit you. Remember that choice of clothing styles is relative. Don't order because you saw some positive comments about the style. Make purchases when you are sure that the style is perfect for you. You can get these images through Google Images or Pinterest. Also, these search engines have great Celtic ideas for modern clothing.

2. Study the dressing style of Celtic nations: Consider knowing a few things about the dressing style of Ireland, Scotland, Wales, Cornwall, Brittany, and Isle of Man, being the six known Celtic nations. Feel free to add their thrilling attires to your wardrobe. While kilts are great for daring men, the Scottish tartan fits most everyday clothing.

3. Opt for choice Celtic ornaments: Celtic jewelry is readily available for purchase online. The iconic Celtic cross would be great if you are a Christian or you want something that emphasizes the Christian faith. Non-Christians or anyone who doesn't like a cross could simply go for the trisilicon or the torque. Again, you can check Wikipedia or other search engines to see available Celtic ornaments.

4. Purchase original Celtic clothing: Don't be in a hurry to purchase your Celtic clothes. Make sure you are looking for quality and affordability. Sites such as Amazon and Etsy house all sorts of Celtic shirts, sweaters, scarves, tee-shirts, and hats. Also, this clothing come with the names and designs of the Celtic nations already listed to pick from.

5. Choose the right shapes and colors: Consider your favorite color and shape before you place orders for Celtic clothes. Most men opt for black and green tartan trousers. But, if such colors do not thrill you, go for what you are comfortable with. The Iron Age Celtic tradition does not allow women to wear trousers. Instead, there are several long and short skirts you can wear as a woman. Again, depending on your favorite color, most women go for green or brown Celtic skirts. Modest dressing with a traditional look is fundamental to the Celtic culture. Also, buttoned-up green, black, or brown vests on collared shirts could spice up your outfit.

6. Opt for the right shoes: It depends on the outlook you want to achieve. Medieval-looking shoes or boots will make you look authentic while green chuck taylors would keep you happy all day. Also, green, black, red, or brown ballet-flat or river-dancing shoes are perfect for most women.

Other Celtic designs for body decoration include shamrocks, dragons, Ogham writing, Celtic cross, and ravens. Feel free to draw or tatoo these designs on your skin.

Traditional Celtic knots and patterns found in art books can be used for modern embellishments. How? Just use the techniques in those art books to embellish your cuffs, collars, pockets, and other finished items. Map out your work before you create the designs or you'll have difficulty creating the required embellishments. No worries. Just follow these guidelines and the whole thing will be very easy for you.

Plan Your Motif

It is easier to start with patch pockets because you can tilt their rectangular shape to fit the design you want to create. So, to get started, you need to collect a hand-sewing needle, sewing thread, a few pins, basting thread, a permanent marking pen, pattern paper, and enough charmeuse to create bias tubes. Next, follow this procedure:

1. Draw or choose your favorite pattern: It is fine if you can get an existing pattern, but, if you don't have one to work with, you'll have to draw your own pattern. Drawing your own pattern will take time but you'll get it right after a few trials. Still, finding knot patterns should be easy because they are readily available

online. Simply use Google Image, Pinterest or other search engines to locate them.

2. Make several copies of your favorite pattern: Don't settle for only a copy of the pattern. No! Remember you will have to adjust the pattern a few times to get the actual shape you want. Should you need to expand the width of a Celtic pattern, just overlap the original pattern with the one already shaped to size. Again, make sure that you align the base and the added pattern.

3. Practice with bias tubes: Take your time to experiment with the tubes to see how the design turns out. Again, don't just focus a single pattern. Try to practice a few patterns to see how fast you are learning the process. Also, pay keen attention to stitching gauge and knitting.

Make The Tubes

Cut out enough seam allowances for the bias tubes or you'll experience sewing difficulties. Since most patch pockets' tubes are 1/4 inch wide, this tip will aid the process of making the tubes.

1. Cut the charmeuse bias 1 1/2 inches wide: Consider your favorite design and the size of the pockets you want to make before you opt for any silk charmeuse fabric. Cut your bias to size once.

2. Remove the stretch: Iron each end of the strips to remove the stretch. However, you need to pull the strip a little bit as you iron to avoid creating other stretch patterns.

3. Sew the tubes: Align the long sides and fold the stripes on the right sides. Stitch 1/4 inch away from the fold but make sure you stretch the fabric a little bit while you are sewing the tubes. Once you're done with this row, stitch another row one inch away from the first one. Afterwards, you feel free to trim the fabric around the stitching line until your desired shape and size is attained.

4. Press the tube flat: Use a tube turner to flatten the right side of the tubes. Again, feel free to use your favorite flattening method if the tube turner does not work for you.

Get a Template Where You Can Stitch the Design

It is time to turn your paper design into a template you could use to map your tubes. Here is what you need to do.

1. Transfer the motif: Place the design on a pattern paper and use a permanent marking pen to trace it. Ensure that the whole design is clear on the paper so that you can see the various crossovers and intersections of the design.

2. Place a tube over the template: Focus more on the panel, not the edges, or you'll end up joining the tubes and the whole thing will be messed up. Pin the template on the tube from the start of an intersection to its end.

3. Baste the tube: Be careful not to stitch the intersection lines of tubes while you baste the tube. Run this process continuously until you baste the whole design.

4. Stitch the intersections: Tack the basted tubes at their intersection points. Ensure that none of the stitches is showing at the other side of the fabric.

5. Finish the panel: Get the basting threads off the template and steam the design for some minutes, and hand-stitch the design to your pocket.

Chapter Summary

- Celtic patterns can be used to decorate trousers, skirts, tops, and jewelry.

- You can download your favorite Celtic patterns online or simply design one from scratch.

The next chapter is all about you mastering your Celtic knots. See you there.↓

Chapter Three:
Master Your Celtic Knots

Celtic knots are beautiful designs that anyone can create in the comfort of their homes. They can be scary if it's your first attempt to draw them. Gradually, as you continue to create these decorative artworks, you will begin to master them and everything will become very easy for you. These knots can enhance your work with little or no effort at all. You really don't have to be an expert at drawing before you can create amazing Celtic knots. No! Just a few guidelines and you'll be good to go. However, to master these Celtic knots, you need to embrace constant practice. Soon, you will learn how to draw some Celtic knots, but before then, pay keen attention to these instructions if you really want to master how to create different Celtic knots.

1. Learn to draw straight lines: Celtic knots involve so many straight lines and there's no way you can master these knots if you still have issues drawing straight lines. So, begin to practice drawing straight lines.

2. Practice drawing different categories of curves: Celtic knots involve several horizontal and vertical curves. You just have to understand how to draw these curves before you can create

your favorite knots. How will you master these curves without constant practice?

3. Learn to vary the width and height of a curve: Celtic knots come in different sizes and shapes, you'll need to either increase or decrease the width and height of your curves. So, the earlier you start learning how to do this, the better it is for you.

4. Begin to visualize in 3D: You need to create a 3D map of the Celtic knots you want to draw. So, if you don't know how to do it, learn it. You can search YouTube for videos on how to create 3D maps of Celtic knots.

5. Visualize overlap, top, and bottom lines: Early planning is good for every task, including Celtic knots. Take your time to visualize how the whole thing will turn out before you start drawing, especially if it is the first time you're creating a Celtic knot. Make sure you decide the lines to overlap and those that will occupy the top and bottom position.

6. Practice shading: Sure, you will have to shade your pattern to reflect your favorite look. Decide in advance the color you want to use. Again, if you're confused on how to properly shade your pattern, feel free to check online videos and tutorials on Celtic knots' shading.

7. Learn to add shadows: While shading the Celtic knot, you might want to create a shadow effect in a particular area of the knot. There are several online aids for people who do not know how to add shadows to their Celtic knots. Find these aids and learn how to do it properly.

Pay keen attention to the above tips if you want to draw faultless Celtic knots.

How to Draw the Celtic Tree of Life Knot

The Celtic tree of life looks complex but you'll have no problem drawing it if you can break it into steps. First, draw the large curly branches before you begin to add the smaller ones. Once everything is set, add the fun, finishing decorative shapes. Here is all you need to create a perfect Celtic tree of life.

Required Materials

- Drawing paper

- Black marker

- Crayons

Instructions

Follow these steps to draw your Celtic tree of life in just an hour:

1. Draw the two curly sides of a tree and add the top curvy branches.

2. Sketch the lower branches and the ground lines before you add the two center branches.

3. Add smaller branches from the bottom of the tree until you get to the top.

4. Add your favorite decorative shapes such as spots, mushrooms, rectangles, and triangles, as well as flowers and other decorations to the ground of the tree.

5. Use the marker to trace the tree before you add color using your crayons.

How to Draw a Celtic Love Knot

Celtic love knot is also known as the heart knot and it represents affections and everlasting love. Follow these steps to draw your own Celtic heart knot in the comfort of your home.

1. Sketch a heart. Right at the top of the heart you'll see the point joining the two sides. Draw two lines down, one for each side, form the point to create a diamond.

2. Create three slightly curved interlocking lines from the diamond.

3. Sketch another heart beside the first heart. Locate the point that joins the two sides at the top and connect the line on the left with the first heart, while the line on the left rests on the right line.

4. Use the slightly curved lines created in Step 2 to form three arrow points. Allow only the line on the right of the other heart to overlap the arrow points.

Make sure there are no line breaks. Keep all your lines straight.

How to Draw Celtic Trinity Knot

Celtic trinity knots are common designs for Christian faithfuls and non-Christians, and you can draw these knots at your comfort by following these simple steps.

1. Draw a dividing line. Place one dot each at top, lower left, and lower right parts of the dividing line.

2. Sketch a big arc at the top dot and let it ache slightly to the left dot and the right of the dividing line.

3. From the top dot, draw another arc and let it ache slightly down towards the left of the dividing line, before it crosses to the right dot.

4. Connect the left and right dots to the big arc to create the trinity knot.

5. Draw another trinity knot on the inside of the dividing line but make sure the width is equal all through.

6. Erase intersecting lines and add your favorite color to spice it up.

How to Draw the Celtic Cross Knot

Celtic cross knot, just like the trinity knot, is a common design for Christians, and it is easy to draw. Feel free to draw your favorite Celtic cross in the comfort of your home by following these steps.

1. Draw a circle that can surround the cross. Take your time to examine the size of the cross before you sketch this circle.

2. Sketch a smaller circle on a parallel line with the first circle.

3. Draw a small circle in the middle of the previous circles.

4. Sketch the arms of the Celtic cross design. Draw divergent horizontal curved lines by the side of the circle in the middle of the previous circles. Join the horizontal lines on each end to form scalloped patterns, before you sketch an L-shaped line on each of the arms. Again, draw a pair of curved and vertically diverged lines to join the scalloped patterns.

5. Sketch another L-shaped line for each horizontal arm, with the line at the base of the arm. Also, draw two divergent curved lines down from the horizontal arms but make sure

that the two lines are longer than the arms. Join all the lines with a scalloped line at the base.

6. Sketch the knot pattern on each horizontal arm, and create two rounded yet opposite teardrop shapes with a few curved lines. Draw a smaller teardrop shape to overlap the opposite ones.

7. Sketch your knot pattern in the horizontal arms. Draw an overlapping teardrop for each knot. Also, sketch the knot pattern at the bottom of the Celtic cross.

8. Erase all overlapping lines and apply your favorite color on the Celtic cross.

What inspires you to create the Celtic knot? Sure, you don't just jump out your bed in the morning to design some Celtic knots without being motivated to do so. Alexander Babich, MacoshDesign manager, confessed that he was inspired to design Celtic knots after he watched an animated film, 'The Secret of Kells.' The main character in the film did some crazy Celtic patterns and designs and Babich was inspired to create his own Celtic designs. He later said that creating Celtic knots is just like solving a puzzle. It can turn out to be complicated, incredible, and amazing. So, just like Babich, you too need to identify the source of your inspiration. Why? Inspiration is what fuels your passion to design your favorite Celtic knots, as well as what keeps you going. So, after you have

identified what inspires you, what is the next step?
Draw your favorite Celtic knot.

Chapter Summary

- Celtic decorative artworks can be designed in the comfort of your home by using determination and creativity.

- Locate what inspires you to create Celtic patterns to make them attractive and appealing.

You just learned how to master Celtic knots. The next chapter captures secret grid techniques for drawing Celtic patterns.↓

Chapter Four:
Secret Grid Technique to Draw Patterns

Apparently, being an intermediate designer, you have already drawn more than a dozen Celtic patterns over the years. But you often ask yourself why some of these patterns were slightly different from what you really wanted to draw. You are not alone. Hundreds of designers face this challenge daily. Still, use the grid method to achieve accuracy in your drawings. Here is all you need to do to apply the grid technique to draw accurate and efficient Celtic patterns.

Required Materials

- A gridded paper

- A black pen

- Pencil

- An eraser

How to Draw the Pattern

1. Draw the grids: The number of grids to draw depends on the Celtic pattern you want to work on. Take your time to carefully consider the shape and size of the pattern. Ensure that the height and length of the pattern carry an equal

number of grids. Still, you may only need to draw 3 overlay grids—primary, secondary, and tertiary grids.

a. Just draw a few dots to create the primary grid but make sure the dots are vertically and horizontally aligned. Besides that, you need to make sure that the dots are evenly spaced. Better still, use a primary grid of 15 dots wide and 5 dots high. Place a dot in the middle of the primary units to create the secondary grid. Find a way to differentiate primary and secondary grids when you are working with a single color.

b. The tertiary grid shows the path of the pattern. It connects the primary and secondary grids to form a diagonal line. Draw the diagonal lines slightly because you will soon erase them. Again, maintain equal space between the diagonal lines and the other two grids.

2. Draw the breaks: Breaks are lines that show the path of the pattern. Practically, these lines appear on the primary or secondary grids but they should be lightly drawn. Follow these rules to draw the breaks appropriately.

c. Just as the outside edges of your primary grid define the boundary of the pattern, they also serve as breaks.

d. Breaks can be vertical or horizontal, not diagonal.

e. Breaks on primary and secondary grids do not always intersect but two primary or two secondary breaks may intersect.

f. Use a pen or pencil to draw the breaks. Feel free to use a single color for the breaks, but make sure that primary and secondary grids do not intersect.

3. Draw the path: Remember that the breaks act as the path. Again, primary and secondary grids must not intersect. Pay keen attention to these tips before you attempt to draw the path.

g. Straighten the path to the tertiary grid but don't hit the break.

h. Trace the path back to the tertiary grid once you have avoided the break.

i. Some break patterns could have rare or strange pathways but don't allow that to mislead you. Use the tips above and you'll have no difficulty creating the path for your primary and secondary grids.

4. Smoothen the path: You will make two turns when you draw the path— 45 and 90 degree turns. The 45 degree turn is a wide one while the 90 degree turn is a little bit light. So, just

try to sharpen the right turns and round over the wide Ines. Again, learn how to follow the path efficiently to create the Celtic pattern efficiently. Still, you can make the path round or smooth automatically while you are drawing the pattern. Feel free to shape the path round or sharp as you want.

5. Erase overlapping lines: It is easy to mess things up at this point especially if you are in haste to erase overlapping lines. Take your time to carefully check where the path crosses a line or when there is a pencil line to erase.

You have just created your pattern.

Why the Grid Drawing Technique?

Grid drawing technique helps you focus on a particular section of an image or pattern at a time. It makes efficient drawing easy, although some designers struggle to use it because they think grid technique is cheating. No! Grid is just one of the practical drawing techniques anyone can use to create complex designs efficiently, and quickly too. Again, designers, like people in other fields, are not magicians. They could opt for drawing techniques that make their jobs effortless. So, with the grid technique, beginner and intermediate Celtic designers can easily create or recreate advanced and complex drawings efficiently in record time. For example, you may experience some difficulties trying to draw a complex Celtic knot. But, with the grid technique, you can break down the knot into smaller manageable segments. Next, you focus on replicating what's in each segment on your drawing paper. Still, grid technique aids speedy completion of great drawing projects. It can help you run many designs in record time and earn higher income.

Using the Grid Technique to Scale Drawings

Use the grid technique to transpose images in a piece of paper to another one. Again, no special drawing ability is required from anyone to use this technique. Just explore these steps to attain great results.

Required Items

- The image to draw

- A scaled drawing paper

- A pencil

- An eraser

- A ruler

- A pen

Instructions

Follow these simple steps to scale your drawings with grid technique

1. Pick your image: Feel free to pick any Celtic knot, but, if you find drawing too difficult, or you haven't worked with the technique before, opt for a simple Celtic pattern.

2. Select your drawing paper: Scale the paper to the size of your image.

3. Mark the edges of the image: Make sure that the marks are evenly spaced.

4. Use a ruler to join opposite marks: Connect the lines to form a grid pattern.

5. Mark the edges of your paper: Again, make sure that the marks are evenly spaced and use your ruler to connect the opposite marks to create a grid pattern similar to the previous one. However, the grid lines and markings on the paper should be lightly drawn because you'll still need to erase them.

6. Assign numbers to each box on the image and paper: From the top-left corner, number each box so that you'll know the image to knit to each box on the drawing paper. Again, press your pencil lightly on the drawing paper because you'll still need to erase the assigned numbers.

7. Begin drawing: Recreate the content of the image on the drawing paper box-by-box. Feel free to start with any box but make sure the

selected image goes to the appropriate box on the drawing paper. Use your pencil to draw throughout because you might have to adjust the drawings.

8. Erase the grid and numbers: Allow the ink to dry completely before you clean the grid and numbers with your eraser.

9. Color the drawing: Feel free to use your favorite color.Yes, you need to decide on the color you want to use. Two or more colors may be used on the drawing but always make sure that you're comfortable with the color for the pattern.

Always focus on the image you are trying to create so that you don't get lost in the process.

Chapter Summary

- Grid drawing technique can help you to attain accuracy when you are creating your sketches.

- Consider the shape and size of your pattern before you draw it before you use the grid technique to sketch it.

- Grid drawing helps you to focus on a particular section of an image or pattern at a time.

In the next chapter you will learn how to design your own Celtic pattern in the comfort of your home. See you there!↓

Chapter Five:
How to Design Your Own Celtic Pattern

You have traced so many drawn patterns on graph papers. Now, you need to go a step further by learning to draw or create Celtic patterns from scratch. Just follow the time-tested steps below to create great Celtic patterns in the comfort of your home.

Required Materials

- Graph paper

- A pencil

- A pen or marker

- An eraser

- Contrasting color marker

Instructions

Follow these steps to draw your own Celtic pattern.

2. Draw your grid: Create a few lines and columns on a staggered grid. Each column and row should be two squares apart but make sure they share the edges. Just count the dots on the

outside edges to now calculate your columns and rows. Also, feel free to vary the number of your columns and rows, but they must be even numbers. Mark dots in the middle of all your grids. Again, use another colored pen to mark dots on the sides of your grids.

3. Sketch a few vertical and horizontal lines: Create a few vertical and horizontal lines on your grid. Make sure that each line covers an even number of columns and rows, while the dot stays in the center of the line. Creativity is required here. So, feel free to up your creative ingenuity to create something amazing and attractive.

4. Connect the dots: Connect the unused dots with diagonal lines but don't join any of the vertical or horizontal lines yet. Next, draw a small arc between the vertical and horizontal lines and the already connected dots. Carefully evaluate how the dots fit into the lines and make sure that four lines are connected to each dot. Join alternating dots to close visible gaps on the pattern. Feel free to use a pen or a marker but you might want to use a pencil because you might make some errors or need to erase some dots or lines.

5. Draw the break lines: A break is a plain weaving design and it enhances the aesthetic layout of the Celtic pattern. Again, break lines

are like barriers embedded into a Celtic pattern to create a super exciting effect. Each break line could be as long as one square in the grid. The few chords that go with these lines must not cross the lines in the pattern. Turn these cords away from the lines to create a closed loop of beautiful patterns. So, how do I include break lines in my Celtic pattern?

a. Be mindful of how you do it because break lines could be wrongly added to a pattern and the whole thing will be messed up. No! Don't be discouraged. You can experiment with it as long as you want but I will give you two simple tips on how to create amazing break lines. Again, the tips will help you save time, effort, and paper, and also come up with an authentic and beautiful pattern. Here are the tips:

b. Position the break line on the edge of each square, directly on the grid line, but make sure that the line starts and stops between the grid lines.

c. Position the break line in the center of each square, between the grid lines, but make sure it starts and stops at the next grid line.

d. There is no fixed rule on how to sketch the break line. It all depends on what you want your pattern to look like. For example, you could sketch your break line downward from the top to create separate sections within the pattern. So, take your time to study the pattern you want to create and tailor your break lines accordingly. Still, you may want to connect two break lines to create certain aesthetic effects. No worries. Create one break line on the edge of a square while the other stays in-between. Don't be tempted to burden your pattern with too many breaks. Repeat your pattern of breaks at reasonable intervals to create an enticing effect. Use a pencil to draw the break lines and don't forget to keep the curves smooth and enticing.

6. Add the curved lines: Stylishly connect the curved lines to the break lines. Here are the techniques to use in drawing smooth curved lines.

   a. Do a 5-minute session of drawing curves for about a week to master free-flow curved lines.

   b. Practice with images similar to the pattern you want to draw. Try to redesign the reference images accurately. Don't be in a hurry - you won't increase your level of expertise until you have done it over and over again. Remember the goal here is to draw an amazing and original pattern you could call your own. Learn new patterns to upgrade your drawing skills and style.

c. Work on a different pattern. See how you can replicate the pattern on your own. You could use the skills you learned while copying previous images but let your own skills begin to evolve. Study the new pattern and structure out a plan to redesign it your own way. Again, feel free to alter a few things about the pattern to make it more charming and attractive. Opt for interesting textures to stay motivated throughout the whole process.

d. Stylishly change the direction of your curves. Curves can be changed quarter-way, half-way, or third-way. Still, the direction of curves depends on the pattern you want to create.

e. Carefully consider the look of the curves before you start to sketch them. Again, be sure nothing disturbs or disrupts easy movement of your arms while you draw the curves. Why? You can't take a break when you are drawing curves.

f. Move your arm faster to draw neat and smooth curves. Fast movement of arms means you'll have minimal control over the curves at first but you'll eventually come up with great and confident lines.

g. Calm your shoulder muscles when you are drawing curves. Tense arms always come up with crooked and tense lines.

h. Consider the direction of your curves. Already, you know that curves play significant roles in the final outlook of a Celtic pattern. So, make sure you turn the curves to the objects they are meant to describe. It's one hard step you'll need to practice consistently to learn how to do it accurately.

7. Decide the shape of your Celtic pattern: Take your time to consider the intended outlook of your pattern to know whether you are still on track. Find out what was wrong with the earlier steps if you realize some things are out of place. However, should everything be in the right shape, create a basic outline on the pattern and fill the negative or empty spaces you come across there.

8. Join break and curved lines: Stylishly connect the break and curved lines to create an outstanding effect on the Celtic pattern.

9. Add finishing touches: Erase the outline and unused dots or lines carefully so that you don't mess things up. Again, feel free to use your favorite color to embellish the pattern.

Now you have completed your very first Celtic pattern. Congratulations! Use the secrets already learned to create different sizes of Celtic patterns.

Chapter Summary

- Make sure your columns and rows are two squares apart when you are designing a Celtic pattern.

- Don't burden your pattern with too many breaks if you don't want to mess it up.

In the next chapter you will learn how to create a Celtic maze pattern.↓

Chapter Six:
Celtic Maze Pattern and Game

Celtic maze patterns are straight spiral lines often used to connect dots. Remember that you connected a few dots when I took you through the process of making some unique Celtic designs. Good! Celtic maze patterns, however, are not that easy. You need to constantly practice how to design the patterns to master them. Do some pre-planning before you try to execute large projects so that you don't mess up the whole thing.

Don't fret because I am going to show you how to draw a Celtic maze pattern straight away. Still, in this chapter, you will also learn several amazing geometric drawing patterns and how to use them to beautify your Celtic artwork. First, let's quickly learn how to draw a Celtic maze pattern.

Required Materials

- A pen

- Some pieces of paper

- Creativity

Instructions

Follow these simple steps to make your Celtic maze pattern:

1. Draw the base shape of your design. To get it right, take your time to examine the pattern you want to create.

2. Sketch internal lines. Carefully add the inner shapes, circles, and other reference lines into the base shape but make sure you harmonize everything.

3. Add a break line. I have already shown you how to handle break lines. Just sketch the break lines on the base lines.

4. Replace the reference lines with curves.

5. Run this pattern on 3 more sides and connect them all together. You'll need to draw a maze-look-alike spiral knot to connect the sides, while the center will have a circular maze pattern.

6. Fill negative space with more patterns and knots.

Great! You have just designed your Celtic maze pattern.

Amazing Geometric Drawing Patterns for Celtic Projects

Shapes such as squares, triangles, and circles are fundamental to all images and designs, including Celtic knots, and they evoke varied meanings. For example, quilters and other drawing experts often use rectangles and squares to represent balance; triangles for energy and stability; hexagon for unity; and circles for protection. Still, these shapes provide perfect aesthetics for Celtic projects. Here, I will give you an array of shapes to create cohesive designs, and also show you how to use these shapes.

Patterns: You already know the importance of patterns in Celtic artwork. So, take your time to create lovely images with patterns. Even a simple shape looks appealing. You can imagine the beauty of a whole image of different shapes. You should carefully select the shapes you need to create a spectacular image landscape. Examine your project and the message you intend before you choose what patterns to use. Again, balance things up. Don't overlap your Celtic artwork with multiple patterns.

1. Patterns with photos: Consider splicing your photos into some patterns to create a striking effect. Paste a few photos of your Celtic knots in some shapes and experience its uniqueness. Shapes personalize images and make them stand out.

2. Lighting and shadows: Feel free to add lighting and shadow effects to your Celtic projects. Create a 3D design and use lighting and shadows to draw attention to particular sections of the Celtic artwork but you need creativity to make it unique. Remember that your level of creativity determines the beauty of your Celtic maze patterns, as well as other Celtic projects.

3. Collage: A collage of different shapes can enhance the aesthetics of your Celtic patterns and make them easy to view on screen. So, create these shapes within your Celtic pattern, and see how your artwork gets massive attention.

4. Diagonals: Use diagonals to help the eye trace your Celtic patterns. Focus on using diagonals to juxtapose the images and colors of your Celtic pattern. In other words, diagonals enhance the aesthetics of your artworks and make them appealing.

5. Isometric patterns: Use the three dimensional isometric patterns to highlight the uniqueness of your Celtic projects. Opt for a hard color if you want to create a striking effect when the image pops up on screen. However, be creative with isometric patterns because it could draw instant and sharp attention to certain words, items, or sections in your design.

6. Patterns with fonts: Combine patterns and typeface to stretch your creativity a bit and move your design capability to another level. Feel free to use different shapes and lines to make your design a little bit edgy or jagged.

7. Patterns within patterns: Sure, your Celtic pattern already has a few shapes. Fine. Consider adding more small shapes within the shapes to make them look complex and beautiful. Feel free to alternate the varieties of shapes for your design but make sure everything is harmonized.

8. Create a theme: Patterns can boost the beauty of Celtic knots. The outlook is better when you connect images to these patterns. It is amazing when the patterns complement one another. So, create a theme for your Celtic pattern. Make sure the images connect well with the borders, colors, and patterns. Create a design that easily becomes your trademark, one that can captivate the most vague minds.

9. Gradients: A cool color design attracts everyone. Don't just go for any color. Use a color that adds value to your artwork. Sure, a gradient background for your Celtic designs will boost its look. Carefully blend shapes together to make your artwork stand out. Still, opt for simplicity. Don't overuse color just

because you want to up the aesthetics of your design. It will mess up the whole thing.

10. Combine many images: Use shapes to mix some images in your Celtic artworks to form collages. See how the images spices up your design and how the shapes complement one another. Still, use only images that are relevant to the Celtic pattern you want to draw.

11. Create overlapping shapes: Feel free to overlap some shapes in your Celtic artwork to create some striking effects. Such shapes could catch the attention of everyone who sees your pattern. Experiment with overlapping shapes in a few Celtic designs and see the beauty such shapes could add to your designs.

12. Harmonize your colors: Opt for compatible colors to balance your Celtic knots. Avoid color riot. Feel free to select any color you want but make sure it is suitable for the pattern. For example, use an orange and deep green color mixture for serious and professional Celtic artworks. A poor color combination will put everyone off your design. Better still, consider how a few colors react together before you mix them for Celtic projects.

13. Make it subtle: Begin to use subtle shapes to adorn or beautify your Celtic artworks. Subtle shapes are not obvious. They work wonders by creating great aesthetic effects in drawings,

paintings, embroideries, and other artworks. Blend a few shapes into the design background to creatively turn your design to a cynosure of all eyes.

14. Do some hands-on patterns: Learn to go traditional by creating personalized hand-drawn patterns. Sure it's hard and time consuming but it's also appealing.

15. Use rare shapes: Do standout designs by using rare shapes and patterns. Don't be compelled to use regular squares, circles, or triangles to design your Celtic artwork. Use shapes that are totally new in the field of designing. Still, the shapes must be suitable for the Celtic knot you want to create.

16. Reduce complex patterns: Don't be tempted to overladen your Celtic artwork with complex patterns. Sure, these patterns add significant beauty to the artwork but they can also trigger loss of attraction. So, know why and when to use them to sustain viewers' attention. Better still, make sure that the complex patterns deserve their place before you use them.

17. Black and white pattern: Some patterns are just great when they appear in black and white, not colored. Also, black-and-white patterns are natural and appealing. So, rather than focusing on colored Celtic patterns all the time, do some

black-and-white natural patterns, and see how charming and appealing they really are.

Don't litter your Celtic artwork with so many patterns. You don't have to bore people with patterns, just because you want to highlight your project with fancy designs. Remember that these patterns can lose their impact when you overuse them. Therefore, carefully consider what your Celtic knot really needs to be charming and appealing. Again, it's up to you to take your Celtic designs to a greater height.

Chapter Summary

- Celtic maze patterns are spiral lines used to connect dots.

- Constant practice can enhance the designs of great Celtic maze patterns.

- Examine your project and the message you want to portray before you choose any pattern.

Chapter Seven captures the special features of medieval illuminated manuscripts and how you can create one.↓

Chapter Seven:
Medieval Illuminated Manuscript

There was an increase in the demand for illuminated manuscripts in European and Arab nations during the Middle Ages. Then, they used beautiful materials such as vellum, silverpoint, and gold leaf to beautify or illuminate the pages of books and manuscripts. Since there were no sewing or quilting machines at that time, the process of illustrating, gilding, or writing the manuscript was done by hand. You need to exhibit a high degree of craftsmanship. Many illuminated manuscripts didn't survive because of the quality of the materials used to design them and the incessant wars in medieval Europe. Those that made it to our present world are treasured, and they expose the customs and practices of the Middle Ages people to us.

Initials of kingdoms sending a message were showcased via illuminated manuscript scrolls in the Medieval period. In this chapter, you will learn how to design or create illuminated manuscripts.

We will write a letter 'A.' All letters share the same concept. Just try to visualize what each letter looks like and adopt the concept of drawing here to create any letter you want. Good. Here's how to create the letter 'A.'

Required Materials

- Cotton paper (hot pressed)

- White gel pen

- A pen

- A ruler

- Pencil and eraser

Instructions

Follow these simple steps to create your own letter 'A.'

1. Draw a grid with a ruler.

2. Use a pencil and ruler to sketch a rough outline of the letter 'A' on the grid.

3. Sketch the letter's confinement box and use your pen to add details of letter 'A' inside the confinement.

4. Highlight the box and letter outlines, and erase the pencil marks.

5. Design the letter in the box and shade with your pencil.

6. Add your favorite color, and highlight the letter with the white gel.

Congratulations. You just designed your own letter 'A' for a medieval illuminated manuscript.

How to Make Illuminated Manuscripts

Writing and painting were done by hand during the Middle Ages, but, as of the 12th century, illustrators began to illuminate their paintings on thin sheets of valuable metals, and this aided the popularity of illuminated manuscripts. The whole process was very stressful in those days but it is great fun today! An afternoon's work is enough to create a story and design it with charming images in the pattern of the medieval illuminated manuscripts. How am I going to do it? No worries because here is how.

Writing the Text

Ready 15 or 20 pieces of thick, white parchment. Cut each piece to 8" by 11" but feel free to decide what is enough for your manuscript. Different types of parchment are readily available in virtually all paper supply stores. Still, opt for parchments that are dusted with pumice powder because their surfaces are rough and receptive to paint and ink. But, should you find no parchment, opt for thick and white cardstocks.

Trim the end of your quill or you won't be able to write with it. Traditionally, the Middle Ages people used feather quills from chickens, ducks, or geese to write text on their illuminated manuscripts. Just get a dried quill from any of these animals, use your scissors to trim the tip a bit to make it pointed, and write with it. Quills are readily available in paper supply stores but feel free to use a fountain pen if you can't get a quill.

Ready a small bowl of black ink, dip the quill's tip into the ink, shake off excess ink from the quill, and start writing your letters on the manuscript. But, if black ink isn't your favorite ink for the project, use the ink you like.

Select the pages you want to write on. Freely write in the top, middle, or bottom portion of the pages you select, or you could just reserve the whole page for images. Again, feel free to create borders around the edges of the pages or draw out where you'll place your drawn pictures. Remember that traditional manuscripts had many large images and fewer words per page. Again, pay keen attention to the first letter on each page to make it larger and more detailed than other letters within the page.

Create your own story or copy one from the Middle Ages. Just make sure that the story you are using depicts fanciful events and heroic achievements. Write the text a few times on a scrap paper to master it. Then, write it on your manuscript. Use calligraphy or some old-fashioned decorative writing aids to create your text and make sure the whole thing appears neat and fancy.

Spread out the manuscript to dry the ink. Usually, black inks on parchment paper can take up to 15 minutes to dry. Let the whole thing dry completely before you move on to the next stage. Also, while quilling the text, keep your hands off the paper or you'll smudge the ink.

Adding Images and Designs

Use the quill and ink to draw your images and designs. Just make sure you mark out your design to know where to fit in the color on the page. Add a few sketches of the scenes of your story and charming images to spice up the manuscript, but allow the ink to dry completely for about 10 minutes before adding new colors. Don't forget that classic illuminated manuscripts had 2D images of fanciful tales as themes, but feel free to create your favorite theme designs.

Sketch a border around your text. The style depends on the look you want to give your illuminated manuscript. Just make sure that the borders are fanciful. Use the quill and black ink to sketch a few flowers, leaves, or vines round the edges of the page to make your manuscript attractive and charming.

Create a base coat for gold leaf, attach a small paint brush to it, press it on your favorite areas on the page, and carefully paint the coat base on the paper. Plasters are used to make base coats and you can get the coats in any of the craft supply stores out there. Feel free to brush excess gold leaf off the page, but you'll have to use a fluffy paint brush to do it. Do you know about gold leaf? It is actually a thin layer of real

real gold, and you can use a paint brush to manipulate it to add majestic lighting to your favorite images.

Use watercolor paints to color your design. Decide the colors to use for the whole image. Dab color to the areas you want to highlight with a paint brush but don't continue the remaining areas until the paint dries off completely. If you are working on this project with your kids, allow them to fill the images with bright-colored paints or glitter glue. Focus on using deep reds, purples, or light greens because they illuminate manuscripts more than other colors. Also, consider using tan or white paint to highlight other objects and figures.

Binding the Pages

Arrange the pages in the right order, cut them to equal sizes, but make sure nothing is missing from the text. Get the left sides of the pages arranged in 3 narrow leather thongs. Spread the thongs across the pages of your book to firmly hold the manuscript. Leather thongs are readily available in craft supply stores but feel free to use synthetic thongs if you can't get leather thongs.

Use lined thread to sew the pages to the thongs. How do I go about this? Pass a thick linen thread through your needle, knot it the end, sew the top of the pages with your leather thongs, and attach all the pages, one after the other, but in a straight line. Doing this can be difficult if your manuscript has too many pages, but you can work one section at a time.

Use wooden boards to loop the leather thongs. Ready two wooden boards but make sure they are larger than your already cut-out pages. Arrange the thongs on the boards, mark their end points, pop out 3 holes with a chisel, pull out the thongs via the holes, and tie them. Use your scissors to cut off excess leather from the book.

Use as much gold leaf as possible and spice up your images with creativity. Again, images on illuminated manuscripts are not always perfect pictures. Just exercise caution if you are using bookbinding tools for the project since they can be tricky to use.

Here are the materials you'll need to do this project.

- 16 to 20 pieces of parchment

- Quill

- Black ink

- Watercolors

- Gold leaf

- Base coat

- Paint brush

- Leather thongs

- Sewing needle

- Chisel

- 2 wooden boards

- Linen thread

Take a bold step to create and illuminate your initials. Just ready some colored pencils, gold crayons, black-felt tip pen, an animated pet or plant, and an 18 cm by 18 cm square piece of paper to get started.

Chapter Summary

- Demand for illuminated manuscripts was high in European and Arab Nations during the Middle Ages.

- Many illuminated manuscripts did not survive at the time because of the quality of the materials and the incessant wars of the period.

In the next chapter, I will take you around the world of Celtic symbols.

Chapter Eight: Celtic Symbols

Celtic patterns are bold, adorable, and appealing but they all have their unique meanings. Each Celtic symbol has a particular message. Today, we will go back in history to carefully study their meanings. So, sit comfortably and relax, while I take you around the world of Celtic symbols.

Celtic Knots

Triquetra

Triquetra is also known as the trinity knot. It is the symbol of the Mother, Maiden, and Crone, a neo-pagan goddess. It uses the moon to showcase the circles of a woman's life. It also symbolizes the three circles of life— life, death, and rebirth; the marital vows of the husband to his wife—love, honor, and protection; the phases of time—past, present, and future; or the family structure—father, mother, and children.

Recently, Christians started using it to propagate 'The Father, The Son, and The Holy Spirit' aspect of faith. Irish jewelry designers regularly incorporate Triquetra into their jewelry pieces to symbolize everlasting love and Irish ancestry.

Square Knot

Square knot is also the shield knot and it has elaborate and complex meanings. It may symbolize the elements of nature—earth, wind, fire, and water; the St. Brigid's four tiers of wisdom—heart, head, hearth, and hand; or the four unique Celtic festivals—Imbolic, Samhain, Lughnasadh, and Bealtaine. Still, the square knot can also symbolize good fortune, prosperity, and protection against witchcraft.

Circular Knot

Circular knots come in different forms and they symbolize purity and wholeness. For example, the five fold symbol, a modern circular knot, has an unseen element which connotes religion. Celts are very religious. Dara knot is another example of a circular knot. 'Doire' is the Irish word for Dara and it means 'oak tree.' Oaks are sacred trees in Celtic culture because they symbolize leadership, power, wisdom, and strength.

Spirals

Single

The single spiral is a common Celtic symbol seen on monuments and other artifacts. It could symbolize growth, balance, progress, connection, and direction. Again, depending on how one uses it, the single spiral could mean a journey from the material world to the cosmic world or the expansion of consciousness, learning, and experiences.

Double

A clockwise movement of two points on a line forms the double spiral and, like the single spiral, it has varied meanings. It is often used to symbolize the sun and its double spiral movement over a year. It may represent balance while one runs two opposing activities at the same time. It may also mean a spiritual symbol of awakening, creation and destruction, or birth and death.

Triple

The triple spiral is an ancient Celtic symbol. It became very popular in 500 BC and its meanings depend on how it is used. It could symbolize motion, energy, progress, cycles, or revolution. Also, the three arms of the spiral can connote, spirit, mind, and body; life, death, and rebirth; father, mother, and children; power, intellect, and love; past, present, and future; or creation, preservation, and destruction, depending on the culture of the place where the triple spiral is used. Still, the triple spiral could symbolize the spiritual, physical, and celestial worlds.

Animal and Trees

Birch and Stag

Birch trees are unique in the Celtic mythology. They can symbolize grace, purity, connections, healing, protection, femininity, and new life. Celts often see the tree as a goddess and they believe that the white bark of the tree could protect people from evil and spiritual attacks. Stag, on the other hand, symbolizes the forest, and it produces antlers, similar to the branches of a tree. It may also mean the deer animal symbol. For the birch people, stag is a male animal symbol, while deer is for the female animal.

Stag often symbolizes empathy, intuition, and extrasensory perception. Stag is a symbol for nature since it is strong, fast, sexually vigorous, and agile. It is believed that birch and stag could boost a person's quality of life. Still, ancient history held that birch trees could protect people from lightning.

So, what's your next birthday? The birch tree is your astrology sign if your birthday falls between 24th December and 21st January. Do you know what this means? People with the astrology sign are movers, risk takers, achievers, passionate, strategists, and innovators.

Rowan and Cat

The rowan tree has many meanings. It is the zodiac sign for people whose birthdays fall between

January 21 and February 17. Such people, according to Celtic culture, are great thinkers. Again, it is widely held that the tree can give humans energy to be creative and original in every task, as well as the capacity to stay positive throughout one's earthly journey. Also, the tree could symbolize death and rebirth if used in funeral rites or protection if placed at gates and doorways. Still, it is a symbol of great blessings, protection, and unwavering insights. So, when something threatens or challenges you, learn to trust your guts and instincts.

Congratulations if your birthday falls under the rowan tree astrological sign. Just know that your attributes will be reinforced by the cat, your animal symbol, and you have nine lives. Still, when people fail to make an impact, you will record great success. Again, your animal symbol makes you fiercely independent and self-reliant but you'll exhibit some forms of mischievousness.

Ash and Snake

The ash tree is a symbol of how the three worlds connect—underworld, earth, and spiritual world. Feel free to call it Tree or Worlds or World Tree. Still, it symbolizes the three phases of time—past, present, and future, as well as protection, greater heights, expansion, and growth. The ash tree is the astrological sign of people whose birthday falls between February 18 and March 17. Although such people are very protective, they have enchanting and endearing personalities. Nion or Nun, the alphabet that represents the ash tree, symbolizes a person's unhindered ability to travel around the three worlds. So, your animal symbol is the snake.

The snake is the Celts' symbol of health and rebirth. It sees beyond the veil that separates the three worlds from one another and it is a source of intuition and uncanny capacity to see beyond difficulties.

Alder and Fox

Alder symbolizes originality and insight. Anyone whose birthday falls between March 18 and April 14 has the alder zodiac sign. The alder tree breeds self-confidence and self-trust and this explains why people with the alder zodiac sign are trailblazers. So, if you fall under this zodiac sign, begin to focus more on the fox, your animal symbol. The fox is so clever and cunning that people or other animals hardly outsmart it.

Willow and Cow

The willow tree symbolizes one who observes life and everything in it. It breeds strength and unwavering determination to overcome obstacles and challenges on the path of one's success. People whose birthday falls between April 15 and May 12 have the willow zodiac sign and they exhibit strong will-power. Should you fall under the willow zodiac sign, your animal symbol is cow, a stubborn and loyal animal. So, as you stay loyal to your goals, you're stubborn enough to face challenges that pop up on the way to your breakthrough.

Hawthorn and Seahorse

The hawthorn tree has good and bad meanings. The thorny crown on Jesus Christ's head before his crucifixion is obtained from the hawthorn tree. The sign is interpreted based on the circumstances of the moment but the tree is usually a symbol of freedom. Hawthorn is your astrological sign if your birthday is between May 13 and June 9. Still, the tree stands for fertility and protection from evil or harm. So, just as your seahorse, your animal symbol, can maneuver the sea despite its high torrents and current, you have the strength to turn difficulties into opportunities. It is widely believed that the seahorse could help you with financial acumen and infallible memory.

Oak and Wren

The oak tree is very significant to the Celts. The Celts say the tree can motivate you to attain greater heights while the Druids see it as a sacred emblem of existence. These people use the tree for wealth and durability spells. Your astrological sign is oak if your birthday falls between June 10 and July 7, and your animal symbol is wren. The oath tree could breed strength and self-reliance. So, just like wren, your animal symbol, you should be industrious, focused, and fortified with strength.

Holly and Horse

The holly tree symbolizes legacy, immortality, prestige, and royalty. It applies to people who are born between July 8 and August 4, and such people found grace with highly dignified personalities. Celts say that holly boughs can ward off evil spirits simply by using them to decorate doorways and gates. Again, many years back, people cut branches off the trees during the winter period and kept them in their houses to provide shelter for fairies, just because they thought holly trees housed fairies. If you fall under the zodiac sign of the holly tree, your animal symbol is horse. Like the horse, believe in your power, stamina, willpower and stubbornness, and make sure you are attaining your goals.

Hazel and Salmon

The hazel tree stands for wisdom, knowledge, and the willpower to attain goals despite the challenges of life. Knowledge here covers formal education and innate intuitiveness. The tree is more about magic wells and springs, and it centers on the universal energy on which all life thrives. Anyone whose birthday is between August 5 and September 1 falls under the zodiac sign of the hazel tree. Salmon, your animal symbol, can go all the way to achieve its goals despite difficult challenges. You, like other hazel tree people, should exhibit this type of commitment.

Vine and Swan

The vine tree stands for balance and people born between September 2 and September 29 always strive to balance things up to make life good for everyone. Remember that balance and harmony work hand-in-hand. So, people with the zodiac sign of the vine tree often develop the gift of prophecy and are unrepentant truth-speakers. Like swan, your animal symbol, don't falter or stop on the path of your goals when obstacles or challenges pile up.

Ivy and Butterfly

The ivy plant grows one step at a time like a baby who's learning to crawl. Anyone whose birthday falls between September 30 and October 27 has the zodiac sign of the ivy tree. Such people rarely take risks unless they are sure things will go their way. Once they make a move, they focus their goals until they achieve them. Know that your animal symbol is the butterfly, known for its survival and transformation. Like the animal symbol, people with the ivy zodiac sign tend to live light-hearted and carefree lifestyles but they always endure life's hardships and challenges.

Reed and Wolf

Anyone whose birthday falls between October 28 and November 4 has the reed zodiac sign and they are versatile in everything they do. Such people have the capacity to refine raw things and make them useful.

They are talented and would surely do well in skill-based careers. It is widely held that the reed plant breeds healing and helps one to build strong ties towards one's family. However, the wolf, your animal symbol, is known for its power, independence, and self-confidence, the same characteristics you need to develop.

Elder and Falcon

The elder tree is also known as the judgment tree. It applies to people who fall under the zodiac sign of the elder tree. The birthday of such people is between November 5 and December 23 and they often end up as judges and jurists. Such people try to remain fair and balanced in everything they do. Again, their passion and desire for justice is innate and they are always willing to render services to other people.

So, if elder is your astrological sign, always remember the falcon or hawk, your animal symbol. Soar higher and aim for greater heights because you have the capacity to see things far ahead of other people. Celtic mythology believes that the falcon could provide direction to people with the elder sign towards achieving their life's goals and pursuits.

Chapter Summary

- Triquetra, also known as the trinity knot, could symbolize life, death, and rebirth of love, honor, and protection.

- Square knot may also symbolize the natural elements of the universe such as Earth, wind, fire, and water.

Next, we will take a look at zoomorphic knotwork animals. See you there!↓

Chapter Nine:
Zoomorphic Knotwork Animals

Celtic artworks are not limited to knots and braids. No. Animals with bodies, limbs, tails, and tongues form a critical part of the Celtic culture. It is little wonder that illuminated manuscripts of the Middle Ages were decorated with birds, dogs, dragons, and all sorts of animals. Ancient books, like the Book of Kells, were illuminated with dazzling and inspiring zoomorphic images and designs, and people still find these books interesting and fulfilling. Almost all jewelry of the period was embellished with beasts and birds. Bestiaries, books on animals, showcased the natural symbolism of animals in the Middle Ages and their supposed spiritual meanings. These books tend to describe the interactions of medieval Europeans with domestic and wild animals, as well as mythical creatures such as unicorns and griffins.

Common zoomorphic animals in medieval Celtic artworks included quadrupeds, birds, and serpents. Dogs and lions were the most designed quadrupeds of the period. But, since the style used in designing these quadrupeds was highly abstract, it is hard to tell which one was a dog or a lion. However, lions and dogs have their personal symbolic attributes. A dog is loyal to its owner and its tongue has some healing powers. Lions symbolize royalty, pride, and strength.

A lion is always vigilant and awake, even when it is sleeping.

Eagles and peacocks are the most designed birds during the Middle Ages. These birds have symbolic meanings in the Celtic tradition. Eagles, for example, symbolize royalty and they are respected for their strength and acute vision. Celtic mythology holds that an eagle is bound to experience an impaired vision when it grows old. Even at that, it gets a renewed strength to fly higher close to the sun. When it eventually gets there, its vision is restored. Again, Celts believed that peacocks have immortal flesh. For them, when peacocks die, their bodies do not decay. So, peacocks became a symbol of everlasting life for the Celtic people.

Snakes and serpents too are amazing zoomorphic knotwork animals. Carefully consider their natural and attractive slender bodies. Again, contorting them into Celtic knots and spirals is quite easy. Snakes could be a good or bad symbol. Remember the event in the garden of Eden. Satan disguised himself as a serpent to tempt Eve. Also, the shedding of the skin of a snake could also symbolize spiritual cleansing or salvation. Ancient legends, beliefs, and the culture of the Celtic people focused on the symbolic meanings of zoomorphic designs.

In this chapter, I will be sharing Celtic myths on the most commonly designed zoomorphic knotwork animals. First, I will take you through the process of integrating a bird knot into your Celtic artwork. Just follow these steps to do it.

Required Materials

- Pencil

- Scale

Instructions

Follow these simple steps to integrate zoomorphic knotwork animals into your Celtic artwork.

1. Use the pencil and scale to sketch a rectangle of 12 cm by 4.5 cm.

2. Sketch a vertical line in the center of the rectangle's longer side.

3. Draw a cross in the middle of the vertical line, 0.5 cm away from the top, to create a block.

4. Sketch the pattern of the zoomorphic knotwork animal on the left and right sides of the block.

   a. Feel free to use a tracing paper if you can't sketch the pattern directly into the artwork. Still, make sure that you use feather-like hands to draw the pattern. Highlight the edges with a water-gel black pen.

b. Don't try to overlap two highlight lines just because you want to balance things up. You may only overlap breaks.

5. Erase rough drawings or pencil lines after you complete highlighting the edges.

6. Add other details into the pattern with your pen.

7. Use light strokes for light highlights or heavy strokes for dark ones.

Congratulations. You just made a Celtic bird knot.

Celtic Myths on Selected Zoomorphic Knotwork Animals

Each zoomorphic knotwork animal had its story and meaning in the Celtic mythology. Some of these myths sound funny or bizarre but the Medieval people attach significant meanings to animals. Here, I will share mystical stories of some of these animals with you.

Celtic Wolf: Wolf was a respected animal in Celtic culture. It was widely believed that wolves nursed one of the most popular kings in ancient Ireland.

Celtic Eagle: Lleu Llaw Gyffes was a legend in Wales. When grown, his wife's lover struck him with a spear, and Lleu turned into an eagle and attempted to fly away to distant lands. But Gwydion, Lleu's foster father and uncle, tracked him down to an oak tree, where Lleu was perching.

Celtic Owl: Gwydion found Lleu and transformed him to his human form. He also transformed Blodeuwedd, Lleu's unfaithful wife, to an owl. Other birds hated her and she had to live or fly in the night. Owls do not come out in broad daylight.

Celtic Boar: The Boar of Benn Gulbain had killed 50 of Finn Mac's men. So, Finn prepared to kill the wild boar to avenge the death of his men. Finn and his men, while trying to hunt the animal, got to a hilltop, where they met Diarmait, but Finn's men ran away when the wild animal was fast approaching. Diarmait stayed behind, killed the boar, and also died there because a curse was on him from childhood to die the day he hunts or kills a boar.

Celtic Salmon: The Salmon of Knowledge went down into the Well of Wisdom to eat up nine hazelnuts that fell into the well. The poet Finegas tried to fish out the Salmon for seven years. When he finally caught it, he told Finn Mac Cool to cook it. However, he warned Finn not to eat any part of the Salmon. Still, Finn placed his thumb on the fish to test if it was thoroughly cooked, and he burned his thumb in the process. Immediately Finn's thumb reached his mouth, Finn obtained the wisdom of the Salmon.

Celtic Raven: The Raven is the symbol of Morrigan, the Celtic Goddess of War, Fate, and Death.

Celts people believe that the goddess determines who would live or die in the battlefield.

Celtic Stag: Deer is the symbol of Cernunnos, the Celtic god of fertility, wealth, animals, life, and the underworld.

Celtic Hare: Osin, a popular Celtic warrior, hunted down a hare and wounded its leg. He tried to approach the animal but saw a door opening on the ground. The door led him into a large hall where a beautiful young woman sat on a throne. The woman had a fresh wound in her leg and she was bleeding.

Celtic Bull: Medb, the Connacht queen, and Ailill, her husband, wanted to steal Donn Cuailnge, the stud bull, in the legendary Cattle Raid of Cooley in Ulster. Cú Chulainn, a teenager, eventually opposed them.

Celtic Bear: Artio was a Celtic Goddess. Celts people portrayed her as a bear and a woman. Also, Arthur of Camelot, the popular warrior-king, was closely linked to the bear. Many Celtic families had their personal animal totem during the Middle Ages.

Celtic Swans: Have you read the myth Children of Lir? Lir got married to Aoibh and she had four children by him. Eventually, Aoibh died and her sister, Aoife married her husband. Lir and the children loved one another so much that Aoife began to feel jealousy. So, she ordered one of her servants to kill the four children but the servant refused. Aoife too could not kill the children but eventually transformed them to swans.

Celtic Horse: According to the Celtic folklore, the puca changes shape and form at will. It could transform into a black horse or a goat, and it often brought good or bad omen for people. Also, the Celtic horse symbolized the Goddess of Epona and Rhiannon.

Celtic Cranes: It was widely believed that three cranes guarded Midir Brí Léith's house, preventing unauthorized access.

Celtic Hind: Sadhbh refused to enter into a relationship withTuatha Dé Danann, a dark druid. Angered by her refusal, the druid cursed her by transforming her into a deer. She was later told that she would be free from her curse if she could set her feet in the dún of Fianna, Ireland. Finn Mac Cool eventually saw her. As soon as he entered Almhuin, her curse was lifted and she became her old self, a beautiful young woman. She later got married to Finn and soon became pregnant. Still, while Finn fought against the Vikings in distant lands, the dark druid disguised as Finn to trick Sadhbh out of the house and changed her to a deer again. For seven year, Finn searched for his wife but didn't find her. He later found Oisin, his young son.

Chapter Summary

- Birds, dogs, dragons, and other animals were critical to Celtic culture in the Middle Ages.

- These animals symbolized many things in the Ancient Celtic tradition. For example, Eagles symbolized royalty while the deer was considered as the Celts' god of fertility and the underworld.

In the next chapter you will learn how to create a double celtic knot paracord.

Chapter Ten:
Double Celtic Knot Paracord

Double Celtic knot paracord is appealing and enchanting, a unique gift for someone who's close to your heart. Design it as a bracelet or a necklace and its uniqueness will amaze you. In this chapter, I will show you how to design a stylish double Celtic knot paracord necklace and you're surely going to like it. The project is simple and fun, and you can make it in the comfort of your home.

Required Materials

- 2 pieces paracords (opt for your favorite color)

- Glue

- Fake ornaments

Instructions

Follow these simple steps to create your own double Celtic knot paracord necklace

1. Loop the left side of both paracords from middle to the back.

2. Fold the other side forward anticlockwise and increase the size of the right loop.

3. Pass the right loop from behind to the right one.

4. Run the ends of the right cords via the left negative space in the left loop.

5. Run the ends again from the front via the middle loop.

6. Pass the ends from behind to the left loop.

7. Pull the pair of ends firmly in the opposite direction.

8. Pass the 4 ends through an artificial diamond bit and cross-loop the two one-color cords.

9. Run the other 2 cords via the cross-looped cords to create another Celtic knot base.

10. Loosen the knot base a bit, pass its ends to the opposite knot via the loop of another color, and cut excess ends and color cord you don't need.

11. Use other cords for the lace of your pendent and stick your jewelry pendant in the center of the Celtic knot.

You just designed a unique double Celtic knot paracord necklace, congratulations.

How to Tie a Celtic Heart Knot Paracord

A Celtic heart knot paracord is an appealing gift of love. It has a dazzling effect on bracelets and necklaces, and you can create it right there in your home. Yes, the process of designing a Celtic heart knot paracord is quite simple. Okay, let me just show you how to create it.

1. Carefully fold the cord to design a simple loop like the heart.

2. Stretch the end of the right cord downward through the loop.

3. Push up the right cord end through the upper loop and relax it down through the lower loop.

4. Run the cord through the down loop while its end goes up through the middle loop and down through the loop at the top.

5. Pinch the knot to form a heart.

How to Tie an Emperor's Snake Knot

An Emperor's snake knot is rarely seen or used but it is charming and appealing. Still, it is one knot everyone wants to tie because of its uniqueness. So, expect to see lots of variations on how people tie it. Yes, that's originality in design. I'll soon show you how to tie the knot but feel free to use it as a standalone, or spice it up as keychains, bracelets, necklaces, or other designs that thrill you. Eager to tie an Emperor's snake knot? Good! Here's how to do it.

First, tie the normal snake knot, add two loops to its side to give it the loop of an Emperor knot. Still, like the regular snake knot, the Emperor's snake knot is a 2 stranded knot.

Instructions

Just follow these simple steps to tie your Emperor's snake knot.

1. Ready 2 strands and use the left end of the strands to create a loop.

2. Run the right end top-down from the loop before it passes behind the left end.

3. Stretch it back to the right loop to design the regular snake knot.

4. Run the right end top-down into the right loop through the back of the right strand.

5. Pass the left end top-down through the left loop close to the front of the left strand.

6. Run the slack to the two ends through the side loops and tighten it up.

Great work! Congratulations. You just learned how to tie an Emperor's snake knot.

What Size of Paracord Do I Need for My Celtic Knot?

Every Celtic project requires planning. Part of this planning is to know how much paracord you need for a particular project. Unfortunately, most guidebooks out there do not come with basic tips on how anyone can plan ahead for their paracord projects. Here, I shall be showing you the amount of paracords you'll need to design a few Celtic knot projects.

Paracord for Bracelets

Running out of cords in the middle of a project is annoying, but this can surely be dealt with. The standing rule for anyone who's designing a cobra weave or any other weave is that they should ready one foot of paracord for one inch of bracelet. Still, this rule may change if your wrists are very large or you intend to design a very wide bracelet. Also, don't forget to ready one and a half feet of paracord for your center strands. A perfect amount of paracord for most bracelets is 10 feet. Here is a rough sketch of the amount of paracord to have ready for 8" wrist bracelets.

- 8 to 10 ft. for cobra

- 8.5 ft. for spiral quick-release.

- 25 ft. for king cobra.

- 8 to 10 ft. for corkscrew or telephone cord.

- 16 to 20 ft. for trilobite.

Paracord for Belts

Belts are longer and wider than all bracelets. So, be prepared to ready tons of cords when you want to design one. Again, the amount of cords for belts depends on the size of your project. You'll need 120 ft. of paracord for a double Cobra belt.

Paracord for Handle Wraps

It is hard to give an estimate of cords to ready for handle wraps. Why? What to use depends on the length and diameter of the project and the method you plan to use. So, calculate the length and diameter of your handle to know the amount of paracord to order. However, to design a West Country Whipping with 1" handle diameter, you'll need 40" paracord per handle inch.

Paracord for Other Designs

Try to have extra paracord ready for complex projects because you will not always find suitable formulas for estimates. Here are some cordage estimates.

- 10 to 15 feet for turks head coaster

- 50 feet water bottle net with sling

- 7 feet leash

- 37 feet 4-strand round braid

How to Conserve Your Paracord

Earlier, I told you that the size of your design and the method you choose to adopt could determine how much paracord you'll use for the project. Still, you can conserve your paracord. How? Pay keen attention to the following tips.

1. Don't detach from the spool during the process of designing a cobra bracelet. Wait until you finish the bracelet if you want to conserve your paracord. So, how can I do this? Make your bracelet cord 4 or 5 feet and slack it at the end of your weaving line. Still, make sure that your standing end goes up when you are weaving. Do you know where the standing end is? Yes, it is the area joined to the spool. With this, you won't need to lift the spool while you're designing a knot.

2. Leave between 3 and 5 feet paracord to practice new knots.

3. Use leftover paracord pieces to design rings, zipper pulls, keychains, and similar designs.

4. Weave 3" projects with scrap pieces of paracord and divide what you used by 3 to know your average cord for one inch.

Still, these tips may not work for all projects because it is hard to estimate the amount of paracord required for all designs. And, most times, a trial-by-error approach is used to determine the pieces of paracord to ready for a project.

Chapter Summary

- A double Celtic knot paracord is a unique gift for someone who is very special to you.

- Carefully consider the size of the paracord you need for a particular project before you start it.

Chapter Eleven is all about Celtic monkey fist and how you can design one. See you there.↓

Chapter Eleven:
Celtic Monkey Fist

Celtic monkey fist is a charming ornamental knot. Many years ago, the Celtic monkey fist knot provided extra weight for the sailor's heaving line, making it easier for sailors to throw their cable to the shore. In this chapter, I will teach you how to design a Celtic monkey fist with or without a marble.

Required Materials

- A pair of scissors

- 4 ft. paracord

- Creativity

Instructions

Follow these simple steps to create your own Celtic monkey fist without marble.

1. Fold one end of your paracord, create a curve in the 'U' side of the cord, and run the end of the paracord through the curve.

2. Trim the excess to shorten the cord and place two fingers on the cord ball— top and down parts of the ball.

3. Muffle the cord twice on those fingers to create 2 curves, run the end of the cord thrice around the curves, and then carefully remove your fingers.

4. Circle the cord over the curves to design a circular curve on the ball and cut trim excess cord off.

Great work so far. You just designed a monkey fist without a marble. Let us move a bit further to design one with a marble.

How to Design a Monkey Fist with a Marble

A few minutes ago, you learned how to design a monkey fist without a marble. Now, I will teach you how to make one with a marble. Still, just like the previous fist, you can create this at the comfort of your home, although you could face some issues during your first few attempts. Here is how to design it.

Required Materials

- A pair of scissors

- Lighter

- 4 ft. paracord

- A marble

- A pointy object

- A bit of patience

Instructions

Follow these simple steps to create your monkey fist with a marble.

1. Fold one end of your paracord, create a loop in the 'U' side of the cord, run the end of the cord through the loop, trim to shorten the cord, and place two fingers on the cord ball— top and down parts.

2. Muffle the cord twice on your two fingers to create 2 loops, run the end of the cord thrice around the loops, and carefully loose your fingers. Circle the cord over the loops to create another circular loop on the ball.

3. Fix the marble in the center of the circular loop, tighten the cord slowly and gradually, and use the pointy object if it is hard to pull the cord.

You just finished making a monkey fist with a marble.

Monkey Fist Keychain

Feel free to design a monkeyfist keychain if you love creating amazing things from rope or paracord. A monkey fist keychain is easy and fun to design, and something you'll want to design from time to time.

Just a few tips and you are on your way to creating beautiful designs, and also teaching other people how to do it. No worries. Here is how to create your monkey's fist keychain in the comfort of your home.

Required Materials

- 3 ft. and 7 inches paracord (any cord or rope could be used)

- A keyring

- 1 bead

Instructions

Follow these simple steps to design your own monkeyfist keychain.

1. Make the monkey fist: First, use one end of your paracord to make a monkey's fist. Instead of paracord, we will use rope for this project. I think you can make a monkey's fist already but no worries if you can't. Here's a reminder of how to do it.

   a. Loosely cloak the rope three times around your fingers.

   b. Swaddle it thrice horizontally and vertically encircling the first three curves loosely.

c. Use a bead or any small round objects to design the core of your monkeyfist. Here, we will use a bead.

d. Muffle the rope three times through the vertical and horizontal gap of the wrappings to encircle the core.

e. Stretch the rope to tighten your monkey fist knot. Just make sure you don't pull the knot's two ends.

2. Create the hangman's noose: Design the hangman's noose and attach your keyring as soon as you finish making your monkey's fist knot. The hangman's noose will sit on the rear side of the rope. Again, create the hangman's noose if you know how to do it, and move to the next step. You can't design it? No worries. Here's how you can create the hangman's noose.

a. Use the rope to make an S-shape and swaddle the end of the monkeyfist all over the rope's three strands.

b. Slip the fist through the curve at that end as soon as the rope is finished and pull out the strand of rope through the other end to tighten the curve that supports the fist.

c. Muffle the strand around the rope to make it very thick and super glue the end of the rope and the beginning of the monkey fist. But, if you choose to use a paracord for another monkey's fist keychain, melt the two ends with a lighter.

   d. Trim excess rope and attach the keyring on the noose end loop.

3. Step 3. Add finishing touches: Feel free to float your monkey fist keychain with some floating ropes. Just make sure what you are using is not as heavy as the core.

You have just designed a monkey fist keychain, congratulations.

Chapter Summary

- Celtic monkey fist is a charming ornamental knot that helps sailors throw their cables to the shore easily.

- You need a little bit of creativity and commitment to create one.

In the next chapter you will learn how to design a Celtic knot keychain.

Chapter Twelve:
Celtic Knot Keychain

Celtic knot designs look pleasing and attractive. Also, they are so simple that you can create them on your own with little or no supervision at all. In this chapter, I will show you how to design a few Celtic knot keychain projects. But, before then, let's quickly create a regular Celtic knot keychain now.

Required Materials

- Five 170 cm polyester cords

- Some safety pins

Instructions

Follow these simple steps to create a regular Celtic knot keychain

1. Mark the cords 10 cm apart, align, and pin them together.

2. Use the last left cord and the right cord closest to it to design a knot.

3. Use the second-to-the-last left cord and the middle cord to create another knot.

4. Repeat the process to tie yet another knot with the last right cord with the left cord closest to it.

5. Run the whole process from left to right until you tie the cords to knots, rotate the cords, and pin everything firmly to create a long chain.

6. Fold and heat the ends to bind them.

Great work. You just designed a regular Celtic knot keychain.

Celtic Knot Keychain Projects

Knotted Leather Earrings

Knotted leather earrings are nice homemade Celtic knots that you can present to your loved ones as gifts. Not only are these earrings simple, stylish, beautiful and charming, you can design them right there in your home with little or no supervision. It'll soon be the season of sending gifts to loved ones and you'll surely need to send some. Yes, creating the knotted leather earrings takes just a few minutes to complete. Beautiful, isn't it? Here's how you can create your own knotted leather earrings.

Required Materials

- Leather

- 7 inches thin leather

- A pair of scissors

- 14 pieces beadalon cord (silver-plaited c-crimp ends)

- 14 pieces 1.9 mm Beadalon c-crimp cord ends

- 60 pieces French hook earring wires (silver-plated)

- 16 pieces Beadalon ear wires (gold-plated ball and spring nickel free)

Instructions

Follow these simple steps to design your own knotted leather earrings.

1. Cut your leather to 3/8" by 4" strips. I think earrings should be small and firm on the ears of people using them, but feel free to vary the size of your strips if you love huge and long earrings.

2. Tie the leather into a simple and loose knot.

3. Bring together the tail ends of the knot and pinch them, leaving the leather's good sides to face out. Lay the c-crimp on the tail ends, hold them with your pliers, and pinch everything firmly.

4. Hold the loop of the c-crimp and clip the earring wire to its top.

5. Trim the longer strips or make the earrings dangle down a bit.

You just designed cute earrings.

Celtic Knot Pendant

People have been using this adorable knot right from the time of the Roman Empire. The Celtic knot pendant is beautiful and charming, but difficult to design. Still, with the few tips here, you will surely create your own Celtic knot pendant. Let's get started!

Required Materials

- AutoCAD

- Pendant image

- A pair of pliers

- 13/16 Craftsman socket

- Trefoil wire

- A triangle file

- Hobby file

Instructions

Follow these simple steps to design your Celtic knot pendant.

1. AutoCAD your image: First, search for your favorite pendant image online, copy, and paste it in your AutoCAD, place three arcs on it, and rotate the arcs till the image takes a circular shape. Use the trim tool to clean it up to get a simple symbol of the pendant you want to design. Check for the circle where the arcs intersect and overlap. Mark the circle.

2. Connect the wire to the circle: Connect the 14-gauge zinc-coated steel wire trefoil to the circle. Just walk in to one of the hardware stores within the neighborhood to buy it. Better still, you can place an online order for trefoil and it will be delivered to your doorstep. Form a coil with the Craftsman socket and your pair of pliers. Ensure that the size of the coil is equal to what you have on the template. Feel free to trim the coil or wind the wire to suit the lengths of the arcs. Also, mark the direction of the curves with a triangle file.

3. File the notches: Just file your notches between 45 and 90 degrees before you try to fold the pendant. Why? You need the whole thing to be neat and straight, don't you?

4. Fold the knot: Carefully bend two, out of the three arcs, together. Open the middle arc to make the arcs look like folded arms and bend in the last arc. Close the wire and open the arc with the pliers and check again to see whether

the socket is well connected for proper reshaping.

5. Weave the circle: Use the socket and pliers method to form the inner circle. Twist the parts of your trefoil a little bit to pave way for threading. Just remember that the joint lies at the back of one of the arcs. Find it.

6. Solder and polish the pendant: Quickly wrap the 16-gauge wire all over your hobby file to make a jump ring, connect the arcs, and solder the joints.

7. Remove any marks on the pendant and use a buffing wheel to polish the pendant.

You just designed a Celtic knot pendant.

Celtic Heart Knot

The Celtic heart knot is unique and adorable. It is cool for decorations or you can use it to design your jewelry. Better still, design a card with this knot, send it to someone who's special to you on Valentine or St. Patrick's Day, but be ready to be forever trapped in a pool of affection. That's the magic strength of the Celtic heart knot. Here is how to tie your own Celtic heart knot.

Required Materials

- Ropes

- Shoelaces

- Paracords

- A pair of scissors

Instructions

Follow these simple steps to tie your own Celtic heart knot.

1. Fold your cord in half to create two loops.

2. Pull the right loop to the top of the cord. Hold the right loop with your thumb and try to secure the left loop too.

3. Pass the left loop below the right one, halfway to the middle-top. Lower the left loop but pay keen attention to where the two loops intertwined. Hold the right cord, weave top, bottom, and back parts.

4. Carefully trim the Celtic knot to shape.

Celtic Knot Macramé Bracelet

The Celtic knot macramé bracelet is charming. Hundreds of years ago, the bracelet was considered as a symbol of devotion and eternal life, while its three adorable intersecting loops symbolized fire, earth, and water—the three natural elements of human existence. Still, the beauty of the Celtic knot macramé bracelet continues to amaze our generation. Yet, it is

so simple that you can design it in a few minutes.
How? No worries. Here is how.

Required Materials

- 72" leather cord (with 1 1/2 or 2 mm thickness)

- 4 or 6 large-hole beads

- Button for clasp

- Clipboard

- Needle and thread

- A pair of scissors

Instructions

Follow these simple steps to design your own
Celtic knot macramé bracelet.

1. Tie the button clasp: Hold the center of cord,
   needle-thread the button, and use an overhand
   knot to tie the button in position.

2. Secure the button: Use your clipboard to clip
   your button-end firmly to the cord.

3. Start knitting: Just follow the steps here to run
   the knotting process.

   a. Tie the Celtic knot first and form a loop
      with the left cord.

b. Pass the right cord over the loop and channel it below the left-hand cord. Find the triangle space over the two cords, directly below the knot where the button is attached. Run the cord on the right through the triangle under the next cord, over the next one, under the next, and like that till you get to the last cord, and pull it through.

c. Adjust the knot to equal the two sides, and also sit the knot close to the overhand knot. Slide and place the first bead close to the knot.

d. Repeat the process to tie more Celtic knots until you have a bracelet that is one inch short of what you actually wanted to design.

4. Add final touches: Tie one more overhand knot to the bracelet, and gently pull it to tighten the Celtic knot. Create a loop by tying another overhand knot that has the same diameter with your button clasp. Run the button through the loop. Cut off the excess ends.

Now you have a finished Celtic knot macramé bracelet. Congratulations if you made it properly! Don't worry if it isn't perfect. This is a hard one! Start the process all over again and practice until you master it.

Here are a few more tips on how to design an effortless Celtic knot macramé bracelet.

1. Should you have issues laying the bracelet flat, pin the loops to a flat surface, and sit the bracelet on the spot all-night.

2. Traditional buttons have holes drilled on them and they are hard to use. But, if you want to use these buttons, just create some space between your first knot and the buttons.

3. Decide whether to use the raw or polished cording. Just know that while it is easier to work with the raw cording, you need to try polished or finished cording a few times to master it. Still, you can use silk cord, hemp, yam, or cotton twine to design your Celtic knot macramé bracelet.

4. Tie the knots near one another and do away with the beads if you want to achieve a more masculine outlook. Would you like to avoid twisting the bracelet? Knot-tie the bracelet in a reversed direction.

Chapter Summary

- Knotted leather earrings are homemade Celtic knot gifts for loved ones.

- a Celtic knot macramé bracelet is a hard project, but rewarding when you get it right.

In the next chapter you will learn a few amazing things about the trinity knot and mandalas.↓

Chapter Thirteen:
Trinity Knot on a Mandala

Lots of things have been said about the Celtic trinity knot—its meanings, uses, and shape. Designing a trinity knot on a mandala is something you'll want to try since you've already designed some amazing projects. Again, mandala projects are unique and colorful, and you can vary their shapes as you like. In this chapter, I will teach you how to create your mandala and how to design a crochet mandala. Let's start with the simple mandala design.

Required Materials

- Paper of any kind, preferably art stock

- Compass

- Gold glitter pen

- White pencil

- An eraser

- White-water gel pen

Instructions

Follow these simple steps to design your own mandala.

1. Lay the paper on a surface.

2. Use the compass and white pencil to sketch a circle on it.

3. Sketch 4 evenly-spaced lines in the circle. Let the lines intersect in the circle's center to create equal angles.

4. Use your pencil to fill inner details.

5. Sketch raw highlights in the circle with the white water gel pen. Do it when you are filling the inner details.

6. Transfer the design to the slice on your mandala.

7. Creatively connect all the designs together from the right part of the circle, one after the other.

8. Use your eraser to clean up the rough outlines.

9. Add theme to the design with the golden glitter pen.

You have just designed your mandala.

How to Design a Crochet Mandala

Here is the colorful crochet mandala. It is beautiful and charming, a perfect gift for someone you really treasure. Right there in your home, you can create your own crochet mandala, and also twist the design as you want so that it is as unique as you. You want to do it straight away? No problems. Just get these materials ready and you'll be good to go.

Required Materials

- Yarn

- Crochet needle

- A pair of scissors

- Yarn or tapestry needle

- Thread (according to yarn or tapestry needle)

- Sewing machine

Instructions

Follow these simple steps to design your own crochet mandala.

2. Get mandala crochet patterns: Be inspired to create a unique crochet mandala. Download inspiring crochet patterns online. Feel free to follow the pattern or design your crochet mandala from the scratch.

3. Decide your yarn colors: Just opt for any yarn color you're okay with. If you want to vary your yarn colors, fine. Sure, that's a good way of creating a colorful effect. Also, you may opt for many colors but don't exceed three.

a. A crochet mandala with four or more colors will lose its uniqueness and you won't like the final product. Still, consider using bright colors to make your mandala vibrant and attractive. Pastels, neutral shades, and other subdued colors are equally good for the project.

b. Yarn colors to alternate to get bright and colorful mandalas are red, yellow, orange, pink, purple, blue, and green. But, if a subdued mandala is your favorite, use aqua, light-pink, brown, light-yellow, or light-blue yarn.

4. Single out your decorative stitches: Use a simple decorative stitch to design your crochet mandala. And, if you like, you can combine the two to create a striking effect. Single or double crochet are the simple stitches options you can bank on. Also, depending on what you want, choose any of these decorative stitches—heart, rosebud, moss, shell, and camel stitches. Still, you can give your crochet mandala some intricate designs. How? Choose some decorative stitches and design them back and forth on your mandala.

5. Step 4. Create the circles: Feel free to make your circles wide or narrow. Just remember that the circles will determine the size of your crochet mandala. Again, your circles depend on

how often you vary the yarn color. Still, after 2 rounds of narrow circles, change the yarn. For wider circles, wait till you have 4 rounds.

a. Also, you may create your favorite pattern for this, just to strike a beautiful balance. To strike this beautiful balance, a 4-round circle of yellow could follow a 2-round circle of blue before you add another 2-round circle of red, but strive to use the pattern that works best for you. Use a slipknot to crochet a ring on the rounds of the mandala and wrap the yarn twice all over your index and middle fingers.

6. Step 5. Double-stitch the crochet: Create 3 crochet chains and wrap them all over the ring eleven times to form a double crochet stitch. Next, double-crochet each circle for eleven times until you attain 12 stitches in the first round. Still, you may decide to run a single crochet all through the first round to make the round a little bit narrow.

a. Gradually, as you expand the circle, feel free to add more stitches but pay keen attention to the pattern you adopted for your crochet mandala. Still, don't let the stitches you are starting with exceed 12 if you don't want to end up with ruffled circles.

7. Slip stitch your circles: Don't leave any circle open when you are designing your crochet

mandala. Slip stitch the opening of each crochet chain once you hit the end of a round. But make sure you attach the hook of the crotchet before the opening of the chain is stitched. Next, cover the stitch with yarn and run it through.

8. Double-crochet the stitch: Use 2 double crochet stitches for each round. But, if you are working with single stitches, just double them. Sustain the stitches through the rounds. Should you desire a narrower round, use a single crochet all through this stage.

9. Switch colors and start another round: Cut the previous yarn 15 cm away from the last stitch, join the new yarn to its base, and align it with the previous stitch. Just use your simple decorative stitch to design the new round.

    a. It all depends on what you want. Your mandala could be large or small. But, if you are trying to replicate the mandala pattern, you'll need to stick to its size. Again, always consider the suitability of your design for what you want to use the mandala for. Opt for smaller mandalas if you're designing them for coasters while larger ones are great for decorative tablecloths and potholders. Just make sure you create rounds that could support the size of your crochet mandala.

10. Weave the end of the yarn: Weave the tail of the round you just completed. Use s different thread colors to stitch the yarn. A tapestry or yarn needle can be used to do the stitching. So, carefully and stylishly sew the tail of the yarn with the rows of stitches you already designed. Adopt the technique you used to weave the end of your yarn in the previous round. Run the yarn through the previous stitch and tie it to firmly hold or secure your crochet mandala. Still, make sure you weave it with your tapestry or yarn needle.

You just designed your own crochet mandala.

Pay keen attention to the weight of your yarn to know the right crochet hook to use for the design. For example, you'll need a 5.5 mm hook for a medium-weighted yarn. Anything short of this could mess up the whole project. But, if you're working with a bulky yarn, make sure the size of your crochet hook is at least 9 mm. How can I know what size of crochet hook I need? Check the label of the yarn.

Use mechanical pencils to trace your mandala patterns. With the fine tip of the pencil, you can easily create delicate and detailed drawings. Opt for pentel clic erasers since they are pen lookalikes and you can easily use these erasers to clean small areas. Also, the erasers are very effective on pencil marks.

Chapter Summary

- Mandala projects are unique, colorful, and you can vary their shapes as you want.

- You can obtain mandala patterns on the internet, or you can design your own.

In the next chapter you will learn how to design khala patterns with color enhancement.↓

Chapter Fourteen: Khala Pattern with Color Enhancement

The khala pattern looks like a triangle. It is actually one of several patterns used in designing Celtic knots. Khala patterns can enhance the aesthetics and make your Celtic knots beautiful and appealing. Yet, beginners and intermediate quilters often say that khala patterns are hard to draw. Sure, crafting nice khala patterns requires a bunch of creativity and dedication. With creativity, you can design the perfect khala pattern for the Celtic project you want to create, while dedication keeps you focused all through the process. No worries. In this chapter, I will teach you how to use colored pencils to draw your own khala pattern.

Required Materials

- Grainy paper

- Water colors

- Water dropper

- Pencil colors

- Synthetic brushes

- Cotton buds

Instructions

Follow these simple steps to draw your khala pattern.

1. Carefully use your brush to sprinkle some drops of water on the grainy paper.

2. Use the dropper to apply purple and blue colors around the edges of your paper. Use your favorite colors if you don't like the ones suggested here.

3. Spread the colors all over the paper to form a few triangles. Also, fill the triangles with matching colors.

4. Use your cotton boards to absorb excess water from the grainy paper so that the colors can sit well on the paper.

5. Draw lines on the paper with your white pencil color. The lines should start from the edges of your paper to the center of the paper.

6. Sketch the shape of the pattern on your paper. Use the black pen to do the drawing and also fill empty space.

7. Shade the pattern with your water and pencil colors. Also, highlight the design with your white charcoal pencil. Remember that drawings sketched with the white charcoal

pencil cannot be erased. So, carefully run this
stage if you want to perfect it.

8. Fill deep details of the pattern with the water
   gel pen. Also, use the water pencils to saturate
   and balance the pattern's embellishments.

9. Use your black charcoal pencil to adorn the
   pattern with shadows to make it look like a 3D
   design.

Congratulations, you just designed your beautiful
colored khala pattern. The design can be used in many
ways. You could turn it to a stencil or simply use it as
a decor. It all depends on what you want to do with it.

How to Organize or Save Your Khala Patterns

Sure, the internet is saturated with lots of khala
patterns you can use to design adorable Celtic
projects. But, most of the time, finding the perfect
pattern can be challenging. Yes, sites like Google and
Pinterest have both good and bad patterns. The thing
is, you'll have to first sort out the bad ones before you
can get the right khala patterns for your Celtic
projects, which is a waste of time. Find a way to
organize and save downloaded khala patterns or the
ones you designed from the scratch. Here, I'll be
showing you three different ways you could organize
and save your khala patterns.

Journals, Books, and Sketchbooks

Simply draw your khala patterns in a blank journal or sketchbook so that you can easily track them. Depending on your preference, you can opt for graph papers, dot-grid journals, or sketchbooks with blank pages. Just make sure that you are using the journals, books, or sketchbooks for khala patterns alone, since that will save you the stress of finding the right patterns for your imminent Celtic projects.

Feel free to create your khala patterns on Post-It-Notes. Just move the patterns to your journal or sketchbook. How? Copy it from where you drew the pattern and paste it in the journal or sketchbook. It is that simple! Sue Jacobs, the first person to share the idea of the Post-It-Notes, affirmed that the Post-It-Notes option is a unique way one can arrange and save one's khala patterns on journals and sketchbooks.

Again, rather than using blank sketchbooks, sketch your khala patterns in pre-printed notebooks with boxes that could be filled with lovely colors. Here are some of these pre-printed notebooks.

- Storyboard notebooks: These notebooks come with printed empty boxes for sketching scenes when a writer prepares a script. Just as writers use the notebooks for scripting purposes, Celtic art designers can use storyboard notebooks to arrange and save their khala patterns in journals and sketchbooks.

- Blank comic book: This is a series of pre-printed comic book panels that can accommodate your khala patterns. Just sketch your khala patterns into the notebook's empty panels, copy the patterns, and paste them into your journals and sketchbooks.

Binders and Plastic Sheets

Downloaded khala patterns can be saved in a binder. It is easy, safe, and quick. So, whether it is a whole sheet of khala patterns or just a few simple khala designs, save them in your binder. When there's a Celtic knot to design, simply open your binder, choose your favorite pattern, and get started with the design.

Feel free to save your khala patterns in plastic card protectors. Again, these protectors are durable and better than regular hole-punched notebooks. Here are the available options for plastic card protectors.

- Full sheet protectors: These protectors are perfect for full-sheet khala patterns.

- Baseball card protectors: These protectors come with index and artist trading cards, and they can be used to design amazing khala patterns. Downloaded khala patterns can be saved on the index or artist trading cards until you need them to create your colorful Celtic patterns.

Ring-Bound Flashcards

There are flash cards and flip cards that you can use to save your khala patterns. It is very easy to add, rearrange, or remove the khala patterns saved on these cards. And, for reference purposes especially when you're sketching your khala patterns, feel free to remove the flash cards from the ring. Visit Amazon or Jetpens to get these flashcards to store your khala patterns.

Chapter Summary

- Khala patterns are used for designing Celtic knots because they are beautiful and appealing.

- You need to be creative to design a perfect khala pattern.